THE CRYPTO INVESTOR

An Intelligent Approach to
Investing in Cryptocurrencies

04.09.2022

THE CRYPTO INVESTOR

AN INTELLIGENT APPROACH TO INVESTING IN CRYPTOCURRENCIES

AMIT KAUSHIK, CFA

NEW DEGREE PRESS

THE CRYPTO INVESTOR
An Intelligent Approach to Investing in Cryptocurrencies
ISBN   978-1-63730-647-5 *Paperback*
            978-1-63730-730-4 *Kindle Ebook*
            978-1-63730-921-6 *Ebook*

To Aparna, the light of my life.

To my parents, Malti and Srikrishna, the rocks of my life.

Agastya and Aryan, my bundles of joy.
And Anoop and Atul, pillars of my strength.

Table of Contents

Introduction

"You can't argue with numbers."

—UNKNOWN

THE MOONSHOT

On September 26, 2017, bitcoin was hovering at about four thousand dollars, a tenfold rise from the beginning of the year. Media and the luminaries of finance and investing had been predicting bitcoin's demise for years now. But, barring a few teething pains, bitcoin was quickly growing into an adult whose market capitalization would later surpass that of JPMorgan Chase, the banking behemoth.

WHAT THE BIT

Bitcoin is peer-to-peer electronic cash, which does not have a central bank controlling its supply and management. It functions in a decentralized manner, similar to how the Internet works. The elevator pitch for Bitcoin was it would replace the centralized financial system run by the Wall Street banks, who a few years earlier had brought the world economy to the brink. That pitch went over well with the radical sort of crowd.

HOW TO MARKET A NEW FINANCIAL SYSTEM

The Wall Street and financial media had typically been negative about Bitcoin, as its creator had boldly proclaimed Bitcoin would upend the world of finance. His statements had alienated investors in traditional assets, but bitcoin had become the dream currency of libertarians, anarchists, and a few drug dealers.

Bitcoin technology relies on the network effect to grow and survive. This means the increase in participants increases the value of the Bitcoin network.

The key obstacle in the beginning of any network's growth is its small size. The networks often grow from peer-to-peer. When the size of the network is small, the growth opportunities are limited. It is only after the network has reached a critical mass it starts growing on its own, like a snowball.

In the beginning, on January 12, 2009, Bitcoin's pseudonymous creator, Satoshi Nakamoto, sent Hal Finney, a computer scientist, his first bitcoin transaction. This transaction created a network of two, but it was not of much value to anyone else. But just like the Internet, as the network size grew into millions, the network became very valuable to the new people joining it, creating a feedback loop leading to further growth in the size of the network.

Either by coincidence or by design, the launch of Bitcoin was timed well in the aftermath of the great financial crisis of 2008. During 2007 and 2008, excessive risk-taking by the Wall Street banks brought the global financial system to the brink of collapse, leading to a global recession that resulted in mass unemployment, hardships, and riots across the world. Once storied investment banks like Lehman Brothers filed for bankruptcy, many other banks and financial institutions had to be bailed out by the US government to the tune of a trillion dollars, shaking people's faith in these institutions, specifically the banks and financial system.

After its launch in January 2009, Bitcoin, with its promise of an alternative banking and payments system to the Wall Street banks, swiftly gained a critical mass of followers who would provide the proof of concept to the world and kickstart a new revolution in the Internet and finance.

However, before 2017, the revolution was still in the radical phase, supported only by a few ardent fans. To become successful, a revolution needs to be adopted by the moderates. The tenfold price rise since the beginning of 2017 had people's attention.

MIKE GOES TO BROOKLYN

In 2017, I worked at Millennium Management, a hedge fund based out of Manhattan, which managed over thirty-five billion dollars in client capital, investing in capital markets worldwide. I did what anyone on Wall Street with a Bloomberg terminal would do. I tapped "Bitcoin" on my terminal and started looking for more information.

I flipped through a few articles, most of which were about bitcoin price action. Then one caught my eye—an interview of Mike Novogratz by Erik Schatzker of Bloomberg News.

Mike Novogratz is a billionaire macro investor who had a long and successful career on Wall Street. Macro investors adopt a big-picture view of the world based on long-term trends in variables such as technological advancement, fiscal and monetary policies of major economies, and demographic changes. These investors ride the market volatility, ignoring the short-term fluctuations in the value of their investments while holding their positions for the longer term.

In the Bloomberg interview, Mike told Erik he got interested in cryptocurrencies such as ether in January 2016. At that time, Mike had decided to go on a meditation camp in the Bay of Bengal in India. But before Mike left for his meditation camp, he went to Brooklyn, New York, to meet his Princeton roommate, Joseph Lubin, who was running a cryptocurrency start-up out of a warehouse. Mike said, "I expected to see Joe, a dog, and one assistant, and I saw thirty dynamic young people crammed in a Bushwick warehouse coding, talking on the phone, and making plans for this revolution."

Joseph Lubin is a cofounder of Ethereum, which is the second most popular crypto protocol after Bitcoin. The cryptocurrency of the Ethereum platform is ether. After listening to Joe for an afternoon about how cryptocurrencies will bring revolutionary changes to the Web, money, and finance, Mike, an instinctive trader, bought nearly a million dollars in ether from Vitalik Buterin, the cofounder and lead programmer of Ethereum. Mike's purchase price was one dollar apiece.

The next day, Mike left for India, where he would spend the next month away from the rest of the world, deep in meditation, without any access to the outside. When Mike came back from his meditation camp one month later, ether had jumped to six dollars, a 500 percent rise.

At the time of Mike's Bloomberg interview, on September 26, 2017, ether was trading at about three hundred dollars, a rise of close to 30,000 percent from Mike's purchase price. Mike's nearly million-dollar investment had turned into a quarter billion dollars.

This shook me out of my torpor.

At the time, the press coverage and proclamations coming from the grandees of the finance and investing world—Jamie Dimon, Warren Buffett, and Charlie Munger—were mostly expletives such as rat poison, scam, fraud, and turd. I realized Bitcoin was touching a raw nerve among many big, important people and decided to dig deeper and find out what the hoopla was all about.

THE PARADIGM SHIFTS

For the next several months, I pored over books and articles on the technology and value proposition of Bitcoin, Ethereum, and other crypto protocols. In addition to having spent more than a decade on Wall Street, I have an engineering background. It did not take me long to figure out bitcoin and ether, and many other cryptocurrencies, were there to stay.

It also dawned on me Wall Street financiers and Silicon Valley technologists had their individual biases when looking at the cryptocurrencies and completely misunderstood each other.

The price volatility also made everyone, including the fans and detractors of bitcoin, look clairvoyant at different times. When prices made parabolic moves, rising by several hundred percent in a matter of a few months, the believers got loudest, telling everyone how right they had been. Then prices would at times crater by 50 to 80 percent, bringing out the naysayers from under their rocks.

THIS STREET DOESN'T GO TO THAT VALLEY

Wall Street mostly deals with mature businesses and public companies that have already proven their worth and have large market capitalization. The stocks and bonds of these businesses are often traded on the public markets, with price discovery in real time when markets are open. Silicon Valley, on the other hand, is focused on the next start-up that will bring a revolution and, in the process, turn their small private investments into billions when these start-ups go public using an initial public offering (IPO) on Wall Street.

When evaluating a business, Wall Street is interested in the future cash flows of the business and uses them to derive the value of the business. This valuation forms the basis of their advice and investments. On the other hand, the focus of Silicon Valley is on the technology and research capabilities of the start-up business and its long-term growth potential based on potential market size and revenue stream, all of which are estimates. A majority of start-ups fail, but a few like Facebook and Uber can bring considerable returns, sometimes to the tune of one-thousand-fold for early investors.

Cryptocurrencies are an anomaly, though. They are still in the early development phase, like start-ups whose potential will be realized in a faraway future, but they are being traded like public securities with a liquid market providing price discovery, as happens on Wall Street.

It is no wonder cryptocurrencies are highly volatile. They cannot be valued using the traditional financial metrics and methods, so the price floats purely on supply and demand. The value is highly uncertain because blockchain is a foundational technology like the Internet. Many of the cryptocurrencies, such as bitcoin and ether, have increasing marginal returns and network effects typical of many Internet companies like Facebook and Uber. We will not know the implications of the network effects of cryptocurrency projects for a long time.

Cryptocurrency technology is well understood by Silicon Valley. Money, markets, and banking are the abodes of Wall Street. Cryptocurrencies are odd in the sense that they are sitting at the intersection of these two different worlds that often do not collaborate on product building.

Silicon Valley is the brash teenager looking to test limits, break things, and revolutionize the world all the time. Wall Street, on the other hand, is the sober, rule-following, boring rich uncle who ensures things work as smoothly as possible.

THE WHOLE IS GREATER THAN THE SUM OF ITS PARTS

Mike Novogratz had experience as a trader and investor from Wall Street. Mike had spent several decades on Wall Street working as a partner at Goldman Sachs and hedge fund manager at Fortress Investment Group. Mike's friend, Joseph Lubin, a tech entrepreneur, was sitting at the heart of a new tech revolution. Mike and Joe together brought a perspective about investing from two different directions, which usually are antagonistic to each other.

That perspective gave Mike a different approach, and I wondered if that mindset was unique or something all of us could learn from. What I found has given me a new framework to look at cryptocurrencies.

WE HAVE BEEN HERE BEFORE

I decided to write this book in mid-2020 when bitcoin was trading around five thousand dollars. At the time of writing this introduction, in March 2021, bitcoin is trading around sixty-four thousand dollars. In the past few months, there has been a small but noticeable move from corporate treasurers, hedge fund managers, and other institutional players into bitcoin. Grayscale Bitcoin Trust, a proxy investment for bitcoin, has seen an inflow of close to thirty billion dollars in the past year.

Many are simply responding to the price rise. In the latest great excitement about bitcoin, JPMorgan Chase has also come out with a bitcoin price target of 146 thousand dollars. This is reminiscent of the sky-high price predictions in 2017 when bitcoin made historical highs. Many on Wall Street, including Goldman Sachs, were planning to start a trading desk dealing in cryptocurrencies. In 2018, once the bitcoin price dropped by more than 80 percent, the investment banks shelved their plans to start cryptocurrency trading desks, and the high bitcoin price targets vanished from the financial media.

But the ground is starting to shift in the investment community in favor of bitcoin. It is seen as a long-term investment to protect portfolios against inflation. It is currently argued by many highly regarded hedge fund managers, such as Paul Tudor Jones, Stanley Druckenmiller, and Anthony Scaramucci, bitcoin provides inflation protection and can take the place of gold in their portfolios. Gold is often thought to provide inflation protection to investor portfolios.

Many people have developed a partial understanding of Bitcoin and its value drivers. This can lead to bad decision-making as the price of bitcoin fluctuates. Imagine investment banks starting a trading desk selling cryptocurrencies to their clients when bitcoin price had crossed sixty-four thousand dollars after advising them against it for the past years when bitcoin price often went below four thousand dollars.

In February 2020, Goldman Sachs published a report on bitcoin advising its wealth management clients bitcoin was not a viable investment. In the coronavirus-driven market mayhem of March 2020, bitcoin dropped below four thousand dollars one last time. One year later, when bitcoin had risen by 1,500 percent and the price touched sixty-four thousand dollars, the financial media publication CNBC reported Goldman Sachs would offer bitcoin and other cryptocurrencies to its wealth management clients.

The only catch is the bitcoin price needs to rise to more than one million dollars for these clients to match the returns between the publication of the first Goldman Sachs report advising against investing in bitcoin and its about-turn one year later into offering its clients bitcoin and other cryptocurrencies.

What makes it even more telling is nothing in the bitcoin software changed between March 2020 and March 2021!

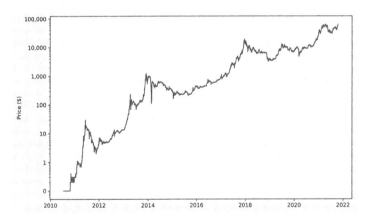

Bitcoin Price (Log Scale)

THE BLIND SPOT MIRROR

To make correct decisions about cryptocurrencies, you need to understand how they sit at the blind spot of technology and finance. You also need to understand it has characteristics of both privately funded start-ups and publicly traded equities. Only then will you make an informed decision about cryptocurrencies, whether you are a service provider, an investment adviser, or an investor.

Due to the early stages of technological development, Bitcoin is still like the earlier versions of the car. It is as if a car engine has been exposed to you without a dashboard, and you are expected to know the working of the internal combustion engine and electrical circuits to make sense of how it works. As more applications are built on top of Bitcoin, Ethereum, and other blockchain networks, there will be better interfaces that allow most people to understand, use, and invest in cryptocurrencies without needing to look into their inner workings.

When I started looking at cryptocurrencies, I realized how difficult it could be to understand them from both the technology and investment perspective. I had to summon my knowledge from education and experience in cryptography, game theory, economics, money and banking, and investment management. My education and experience in engineering and finance came in handy in unraveling the complexities that arise when one starts looking at cryptocurrencies as an investment.

After I fell down the Bitcoin rabbit hole, I decided to leave my job at Millennium Management in early 2018. I spent the next four years building an investment management firm that invests and trades in cryptocurrencies. Building an investment business in this space requires spending countless hours speaking and working with technologists, institutional investors, fund service providers, securities lawyers, start-ups, exchanges, OTC desks, and research companies focused on this space.

THIS BOOK OF WHY

In this book, I have distilled my experiences and knowledge about cryptocurrency investing. I have gained this knowledge through laying the groundwork in this space for the past three years, using the foundation provided to me by over a decade at the elite financial firms like Millennium Management, Barclays, and Bank of America Merrill Lynch.

This book will help you learn about the current debates regarding cryptocurrencies raging in the investment community. We will delve deeper into the what and why of these debates and then present a framework that reconciles seemingly rival arguments. It is essential to understand these debates and resolve them to make an intelligent case about investing in cryptocurrencies.

Blockchain and their cryptocurrencies are foundational technologies like electricity and the Internet. Drawing parallels with the Internet, the book shows how you can make predictions about the future of blockchain technologies. Unlike the early Internet, in the case of blockchain, you can invest in the underlying cryptocurrencies, getting exposure to the future of the whole ecosystem itself.

The theme of disruptive innovation in this book explores why decentralization achieved in a trustless manner is valuable. Most people see the value of trustless decentralization brought by public blockchains from a privacy or freedom perspective. We need to identify the economic value of such decentralization. Only then will we have a better framework to evaluate public blockchains, cryptocurrencies, and start-ups in this space. We will also learn about the basics of the technology behind cryptocurrencies in a nontechnical and accessible manner sufficient for an investor. The book will close by providing specific guidance to different decision-makers and investors about cryptocurrency investing.

In a new and technically complex asset class, there is no clear demarcation between basic and advanced. Basic questions of the valuation may become advanced debates in the case of cryptocurrencies. This book is intended for an audience that wants a full grasp of cryptocurrencies from the perspective of finance and investing.

AND NOW ABOUT YOU

This book will help company CFOs diversifying their treasury holdings into cryptocurrencies, CIOs expanding into this exciting and new asset class, start-up founders, and venture capitalists making better arguments about the value proposition of blockchain and cryptocurrencies. This book digs deep into the primary value drivers of this technology, so it will also help the retail investors trying to wrap their heads around how to benefit from this opportunity that would otherwise only be available to top venture capital firms.

We are still in the early innings of this revolutionary technology. Those who are willing to invest their time in developing a balanced perspective on Bitcoin and cryptocurrency technology and investing may see great career advancements and financial riches.

Book Structure

This book is divided into five sections. Each section tackles a different aspect of cryptocurrency investing, where you will assume the hats of different experts.

Section One introduces the history of Bitcoin and how it is a significant milestone on the growth of the Internet, whose seeds were sown in the 1960s.

In Section Two, you wear the hat of a techie and understand key details behind blockchain technologies. It is not important you understand every concept discussed in this section. As an investor, you need to have a general understanding of blockchain technology. If you find this section difficult, feel free to skim through it.

In Section Three, you will be the venture capital analyst who will develop scenarios of potential paths each blockchain project might take.

Section Four introduces the concept of financial valuation and how it can apply to early-stage start-ups such as block-chain projects.

Section Five brings all of the learnings together and teaches you how to allocate a portion of your portfolio to cryptocurrencies and maximize the returns while accounting for the risk of these investments, also known as risk-adjusted returns.

Even though no previous knowledge of the concepts introduced here is expected, people with a technical background might find Section Two easier than, say, Section Five. I have written these sections with the diversity of the background of my readers in mind. So, if you feel intimidated by a particular section, you can skim through it, retain key ideas—even if you don't feel you understand them—and move to the next section. As an investor, you are not expected to become an expert in any particular area. By developing a familiarity with all aspects of cryptocurrencies and investing in them, you will have tools that help you dig deeper into your area of interest.

There are new concepts in the context of cryptocurrencies that have been introduced in Sections Three through Five. I am sure even if you are an expert in these areas, you will learn from these concepts and research presented in Section Five as it pertains to creating a portfolio of cryptocurrencies for long-term success.

PART 1

THE HISTORIAN

History gives perspective. Over the past decade, many investors missed taking advantage of the growth in the tech sector, including bitcoin and other cryptocurrencies. This section provides a foundation on which crypto technology is built.

By the end of this section, you will learn:

- How tech start-ups grow into publicly traded companies.
- How bitcoin is perceived by the two ends of the investing world.
- How we got here—a story of the Internet.

CHAPTER 1

Where Silicon Valley Meets Wall Street

———

"You never change things by fighting the existing reality. To change something, build a new model that makes the existing model obsolete."

—BUCKMINSTER FULLER, AMERICAN FUTURIST

The dual engines of the American economy and innovation in the last few decades have been Wall Street and Silicon Valley. On the west coast of the United States lies the San Francisco Bay Area, which serves as the global headquarters of the high-tech industry. Home to tech giants such as Facebook, Google, Apple, Netflix, Intel, and eBay, the valley revolutionized almost every aspect of our lives. These companies represent the part of the American dream where a couple of friends working in their dorm room or parent's garage could start companies, also known as start-ups, that change the world. In the process, these start-ups turned from nothing into multi-billion-dollar corporations through various stages of financing, from private pools of money, also known as venture capital (VC), to public stock markets.

Venture capital is backed by a small group of investors who provide money to a company early in its life to fund its growth. Going public allows a company to issue stock, which gives a stockholder ownership of a small part of the company.

On the east coast of the United States lies Wall Street. Wall Street is home to stock exchange behemoths such as the New York Stock Exchange (NYSE) and NASDAQ and the investment banks such as JPMorgan Chase, Goldman Sachs, and Morgan Stanley. These financial giants grease the wheels of American capitalism and play an important role in the supremacy and success of not only the United States but globalization and democracy around the world.

The journey of the start-ups is financed by the VCs, whose objective is to someday take these companies public on Wall Street when their stocks start trading on one of the stock exchanges. This is a long journey in a start-up's life, often spanning five to ten years. The end of the road where the start-up becomes a publicly traded company is when VCs move out of these start-ups' lives and Wall Street takes over. The transition is often smooth and highly profitable to both sides.

Bitcoin, born in the aftermath of the global financial crisis of 2008, aimed to disintermediate Wall Street. In one shot, the start-up techies attacked the payment and currency system and intermediary institutions, such as banks. Until then, the two sides of financing companies—VCs and Wall Street—existed side by side, oblivious to the existence of the other. Their models broke down with Bitcoin. The techies' world of start-ups with their disruptive innovations had come to the gates of Wall Street. A new model of thinking is needed to analyze this world.

In the rest of this chapter, we will explore the mindset that drives these two sides to understand how blockchain technology sent shockwaves through the world of finance and technology and fundamentally **shapes human interactions** of the **future.**

THE FACEBOOK STORY: FROM A HARVARD DORM ROOM TO NASDAQ

According to a *Rolling Stone* article, on a Tuesday night, nineteen-year-old Mark Zuckerberg sat alone in his Harvard dorm room after being dumped by his girlfriend, and he wrote on his blog, "Jessica A—is a bitch." He planned to do some coding to take his mind off her. For the next several hours, in the silence of a dorm night, beer, sheer brilliance, and a jilted lover's desire for revenge competed, and Zuckerberg created a website, Facemash.

To create Facemash, Zuckerberg downloaded pictures of students from the Harvard database and put each of them next to an animal, asking peers to rank the two based on attractiveness. The site accumulated new users quickly, and in just a few hours, more than four hundred students signed up. The site's pages were viewed over twenty-two thousand times that night before Harvard took it down, reprimanding Zuckerberg for copyright infringement and misuse of the Harvard computer network.

Six months later, in February 2004, Zuckerberg, looking to make amends with the Harvard community, created TheFaceBook.com. Zuckerberg told *The Harvard Crimson* he was frustrated with Harvard's progress in completing "thefacebook" project, which would work as a centralized online directory including student information and profiles. Zuckerberg's previous project, Facemash, took information about the students, such as their pictures, from the Harvard database. To avoid copyright infringement issues, thefacebook project asked students to upload their information on a website run external to Harvard (Claire, 2010).

Mark Zuckerberg also recruited his dorm roommate, Eduardo Saverin. Each of them put in one thousand dollars to support the expenses from running the website, such as computer server costs, and decided to divide the ownership between them, with Zuckerberg owning two-thirds of the company. The founders' investments meant thefacebook was valued at two thousand dollars in February 2004.

Thefacebook website had over twelve hundred users within a few hours of its launch. The website was a convenient place to pull out information about fellow students, such as their contact details, the courses they were taking, and their interests. This information helped form study groups and common interest groups.

Mark Zuckerberg wanted the website to remain exclusive. He first opened it to other Ivy Leagues, but by the end of March, it spread like wildfire across campuses in the United States.

The success of the website brought its own issues. The first and foremost was the cost of running the website, as larger user traffic required a larger number of computer servers. Supporting so many users who were not paying for their use of the website was a costly business for a couple of schoolkids.

By summer 2004, Facebook founders were introduced to the Silicon Valley VC, Peter Thiel. Thiel was one of the cofounders of PayPal, which included Tesla's Elon Musk, among others, who were together known as the PayPal Mafia.

Peter Thiel put half a million dollars in Facebook for an ownership stake of about 10 percent. This valued Facebook at about five million dollars. The investment was in convertible debt, which meant the debt would convert to equity if Facebook reached 1.5 million users by the end of 2004. Facebook narrowly missed the target, but Thiel let the debt convert to equity anyway.

Thiel told David Kirkpatrick, author of *The Facebook Effect*, "I was comfortable with them pursuing their original vision. It was a very reasonable valuation. I thought it was going to be a pretty safe investment."

Over the next decade, the Facebook userbase would grow close to one billion. The users on the website would share their contact details, intimate moments, personal stories, pictures, and videos. In other words, Facebook had access to a trove of information to profile its users in intricate detail. The advertisers would mine the information to provide targeted messaging to the users on the Facebook platform, generating billions of dollars for Facebook in advertising revenue.

As Facebook grew its userbase, it continued to attract VC money. Facebook would raise 12.7 million dollars in April 2005 from Accel at the valuation of ninety-eight million dollars. In April 2006, a group of venture investors put 27.5 million dollars at a valuation of five hundred million dollars. Later in October 2007, Microsoft bought 1.6 percent Facebook shares for 240 million dollars, valuing Facebook at fifteen billion dollars. Facebook became profitable only in 2009 at 290 million dollars on revenue of 777 million dollars.

In February 2012, Facebook filed for an IPO led by major Wall Street banks such as Morgan Stanley, JPMorgan Chase, and Goldman Sachs. An IPO meant Facebook stock would become publicly traded, and the ownership of the company would move from private investors to the public holding the Facebook stocks.

The IPO raised sixteen billion dollars for Facebook, making it the third largest in history behind General Motors and Visa. Facebook was valued at 104 billion dollars at the time of IPO, the largest in United States history (Rusli, 2012).

According to CNN Business, Peter Thiel sold his stake in Facebook in 2012, turning his initial investment of five hundred thousand dollars into more than one billion dollars in cash—a two-thousand-fold return.

Mark Zuckerberg was worth nineteen billion dollars at the time of the IPO.

CAPITALISM IN LESS THAN THREE HUNDRED WORDS

Facebook's journey from the dorm room of Mark Zuckerberg will continue through tremendous growth supported by VC investments and reach the pinnacle of success through a Wall Street IPO. The VCs would invest in the company based primarily on its future prospects. The Wall Street IPO would be a result of the company becoming a strong profit-making engine with a proven business model.

The start-ups are born out of the fancies of would-be entrepreneurs. These are highly risky ventures, which in the beginning are often not more than a business plan on a PowerPoint. These business plans chase the venture capitalists who will provide them money in exchange for a chunk of the company ownership. The entrepreneurs use this seed money to build a minimum viable product (MVP), which has just enough features to attract early customers. The entrepreneur then raises more money from the investors to build the next phase of the product, and thus, the cycle of growth followed by VC funding begins.

The investment bankers on Wall Street and the entrepreneurs and VCs in Silicon Valley are not only thousands of miles away geographically; even though both sides are involved in the financing of a business, they are worlds apart. VCs focus on the early-stage growth of start-ups. In contrast, the Wall Street bankers assist large, private companies go public, provide trading in their stocks, and help with follow-up financing through raising debt and equity capital.

The two sides share a brief intersection when the start-up financed by the VCs goes public. For decades, the two were happy to play their roles, not venturing into the other's domain until the disruption to Wall Street came in the form of blockchain technology.

CHAPTER 2

Bitcoin vs. Bitcoin

———

"Put all your eggs in one basket."

—MARC ANDREESSEN

It is no wonder even though both the VCs and Wall Street are in the business of financing companies, their tools and methods are different because each deals with different stages of the life cycle of a company. This was never a problem until bitcoin, and other cryptocurrencies arrived on the scene.

BITCOIN: THE PUBLICLY TRADED, TRILLION-DOLLAR START-UP

On October 21, 2021, market capitalization—the total market value of bitcoin's circulating supply—was over 1.1 trillion dollars. There are only four companies in the US—Apple, Microsoft, Alphabet (Google), and Amazon—which have a higher market cap than bitcoin.

Cryptocurrencies are the native assets of blockchain networks in the early stages of development, just like the tech start-ups of Silicon Valley. However, unlike the start-ups of the past, these assets are traded on cryptocurrency exchanges like Coinbase and Binance twenty-four-seven, and many of them have deep and liquid markets like stocks of large companies such as Facebook and Amazon. Chicago Mercantile Exchange (CME) has listed futures and options on bitcoin and ether. Options on bitcoin and ether can also be traded on Deribit. All of these financial products put cryptocurrencies in the ambit of the Wall Street financiers. Therein lies the conflict.

It is important to know the nature of cryptocurrencies as investments standing at the intersection of two different investing worlds. You need to understand the worldviews of the two sides and reconcile any contradictions before you start to comprehend cryptocurrencies as a new and attractive asset class. The two seemingly opposing aspects faced by investors in start-ups and public markets are critical to investing in cryptocurrencies, as they have elements of both.

WHAT IS BITCOIN?

In this chapter, we will compare those two views to create a holistic understanding of bitcoin and other cryptocurrencies. However, first, you need to understand Bitcoin.

To understand Bitcoin in the most intuitive manner, let's take a simplified view of the modern banking system. The modern banking system is based on a central bank such as the Federal Reserve in the United States, which oversees the deposit-taking banks such as JPMorgan Chase and Bank of America (Mehrling, 2021).

Suppose you have a bank account with, say, JPMorgan Chase, and I have a bank account with Bank of America. Both of these banks have an account at the central bank.

When you look at your bank account details on your bank's website, you see a summary of the account. Additionally, **your account provides you statements, which are timestamped entries of all the transactions you have made.**

To manage accounts of a large number of customers, each bank creates a ledger, which is a record of all transactions the customers of the bank have made. In turn, the central bank also has a ledger that records transactions in the accounts of all the banks it oversees.

Assume I send you ten dollars. This starts a transaction between you and me through the bank intermediaries. The steps to complete the transaction could be as follows:

A timestamped debit entry is made into my account by my bank, Bank of America. A timestamped credit entry is made in your bank account at JPMorgan Chase. The transaction is settled between the two banks once the ledger at the central bank updates the entries for both the banks.

In summary, the ledger at the central bank is the final source of truth and includes records of all the transactions made through the banks it oversees. In our transaction, no actual cash moved. The whole transaction took place through updating digital ledgers at various banks.

In the banking system described, **it is the central bank that created (minted or mined) the money** you and I exchanged through the banking system. **The primary role deposit-taking banks play in these transactions is to correctly update their ledgers.**

The banking system described above is a centralized banking system where money is created, and all the transactions are settled through the central bank.

Think of Bitcoin with capital "B" as the central bank, which holds a ledger of all the transactions made in bitcoin with a small letter "b." A major difference between the banking system described above and Bitcoin is that anyone can hold a copy of the bitcoin ledger. There is no central entity involved. The bitcoin ledger is organized as timestamped blocks of transactions added to the ledger roughly every ten minutes. This structure of the ledger gives it the name "**blockchain**."

The Bitcoin network is a collection of computers that run Bitcoin software and hold a copy of bitcoin ledger, the blockchain. These computers are also called "**nodes**."

You might wonder how the Bitcoin network updates all the copies of the blockchain, which are held by individual participants in the Bitcoin network. Remember, **in the Bitcoin network, every participating node (or computer) keeps its own copy of the blockchain. There is no central entity holding a master copy.**

To update the blockchain in the Bitcoin network, the nodes compete to win a lottery. In this competition, each node tries to solve a difficult puzzle whose answer can only be guessed. This ensures a solution is arrived at only by making a large number of guesses, ensuring the winner has done a significant amount of work, also known as the **proof of work (POW)**.

The winner of the lottery gets to propose the next block on the blockchain by transmitting it to the network. This transmitted block includes a list of currently pending transactions on the network. This block can, for example, include a transaction between you and me. The nodes in the Bitcoin network validate the transaction included in the proposed block against their local copy of the blockchain. Remember, the blockchain is a full history of all the bitcoin transactions ever made. This allows each node to confirm I own the bitcoins I wish to send to you. The **timestamping** of transactions and blocks ensures I can't send the same bitcoin twice, known as a **double-spending problem** because if I tried, the latter transaction would be invalidated by the network participants, as their copy of the ledger would show the bitcoin was already spent. When a majority of the nodes come to a consensus by validating and confirming the block, all nodes in the network add it to their copy of the blockchain. Just like that, all the copies of the Bitcoin blockchain in the network come in sync.

Further, the lottery winner also gets to add a new transaction in the block it proposes. This transaction is made to the lottery winner itself and includes a predefined number of new bitcoins. This is how new bitcoins are **minted**.

You can see the proof of work (POW) is used to achieve consensus in the network as well as mint new bitcoins.

The total number of bitcoins that will ever be minted is twenty-one million. This means the rate of new bitcoin creation has to go down with time. To accomplish this, the Bitcoin protocol code reduces in half the miners' reward about every 4.5 years, an event known as bitcoin **halving**.

The upper limit of the total number of bitcoins that will ever be minted—twenty-one million—provides bitcoins scarcity. The fiat currencies are printed by the central banks as much as they wish. Bitcoin supply is limited and capped by computer code, which is transparent to everyone and can't be changed by any one person. **This is what causes scarcity in bitcoin.**

You can see why Bitcoin is called a peer-to-peer electronic cash system based on a distributed and decentralized ledger called blockchain. It is peer-to-peer because no intermediary, such as the bank, is required to complete the transaction. It is completely electronic, as no physical equivalent of bitcoin exists. It is decentralized because no third party, such as a central bank, is needed to ensure honesty and provide trust in the system. **This is why this system is also called trustless.**

With this, you now know most of what Bitcoin is. In later chapters, we will dig deeper into different aspects of this technology.

WHAT IS BITCOIN: SILICON VALLEY VIEW

In this section, we will look at what qualities of cryptocurrency technology make it attractive for Silicon Valley companies to build products based upon them.

LOW TRANSACTION FEE

One significant advantage of bitcoin over fiat currencies is its design leads to a meager cost of transactions between two parties. This can be very useful in building new financial services. We will see in later chapters the current financial system has high costs of delivering services. So, a reduction of cost provided by blockchain technology can bring disruption to the financial industry.

According to the news website Cointelegraph, in April 2020, Bitfinex, a large crypto exchange, moved 146 thousand bitcoins, about 1.1 billion dollars at the time. According to Paolo Ardoino, Bitfinex CTO, Bitfinex paid sixty-eight cents for the whole transaction.

Compare this to the wire fee in the currency financial system. Many banks charge ten to thirty dollars for wires. This shows how expensive the current financial system is compared to the Bitcoin network.

BITCOIN AS A SOLUTION FOR MICROPAYMENTS

A bitcoin is, by design, divisible into one hundred million pieces. This level of divisibility allows bitcoin to be used for micropayments, making it very cheap to exchange small amounts of currency between various parties. Contrast this with the current system of payments. The minimum size allowed by physical cash is one cent. Even though electronic payments and transfers can happen in smaller increments than one cent, the cost of such transfers prohibits banks and intermediaries from providing such a service.

Marc Andreessen, in his influential *New York Times* article titled "Why Bitcoin Matters," wrote, "Micropayments have never been feasible, despite twenty years of attempts, because it is not cost-effective to run small payments (think one dollar and below, down to pennies or fractions of a penny) through the existing credit/debit and banking systems. The fee structure of those systems makes that nonviable."

The fixed minimum size of payment makes the exchange of small values impossible and undercuts economic activity. Take, for example, newspaper walls. Newspapers work on a subscription model where the buyer is paying for the whole content. If someone is only interested in reading about the markets, they still have to pay for the rest of the content. This excludes many readers who find the price of the full paper too high. Newspapers are forced to charge full subscription fees because reducing the size of the subscriptions per article will cut into their margins as banks and other intermediaries charge them a fixed cost due to their own high cost of accounting and compliance.

The cost of moving bitcoins can be close to zero. The lowest denomination of bitcoin is a satoshi, which is a one-hundred-millionth of a bitcoin. This means there is a very low limit to how small the payment can be. Using Bitcoin, you could send someone a thousandth of a penny, anywhere in the world, almost for free. Small payment sizes can unlock a plethora of economic activity. This will not only increase the usage of bitcoin but also impact economic growth in a positive and significant manner. Newspaper articles, for example, could charge per article instead of taking an all-or-nothing approach to subscriptions. Suddenly, they would have a large number of paying readers.

BITCOIN AS A DIGITAL NATIVE CURRENCY

Bitcoin is native to the Internet infrastructure, meaning it is created, transacted, and lives on the blockchain. This nativity makes it very powerful when it comes to storing and exchanging valuable digital goods. These goods can be money, identities, legal documents, and more.

Given how costly it is for banks to serve their customers, about 1.7 billion people worldwide do not have bank accounts.

It is no surprise Netflix, a completely online service, is only available in about forty countries. If Netflix could charge in bitcoins, its total addressable market (TAM) would explode, as there are more than one hundred fifty countries it could serve.

Anyone with a computing device on the Internet can buy, store, and transfer bitcoins. It is difficult for large swathes of the world to open bank accounts because banks have a high servicing cost per account. Many countries don't even have stable currencies, including Zimbabwe, Venezuela, and Argentina. Bitcoin makes it possible for their populations to receive and keep remittances from abroad without worrying about the loss of value due to hyperinflation in their home currencies.

BITCOIN IS THE FOUNDATION OF NEW WEB

As we will see in a later chapter, the network effect and increasing marginal returns of the network-based foundational technologies do not only solve some of the existing problems in the society but also open up many new opportunities. This happened with railroads in the early nineteenth century, the telephone in the mid-twentieth century, and the Web at the end of the twentieth century.

The first version of the Web was kickstarted by the Netscape Navigator, and it was based on the idea of sharing data. In the early stages of the Internet, leading voices in finance and Silicon Valley were unsure of what value, if any, a data-sharing ecosystem such as the Internet would bring. Two and half decades later, the world business is dominated by companies like Google, Amazon, Netflix, and Facebook.

Bitcoin is often called Web 3.0's precursor. In addition to sending data over the wire, as previous versions of Web did, bitcoin shares both data and value. With bitcoin and other cryptocurrencies, you can transmit data and value in a tamper-resistant manner. We will see in later chapters the core ideas behind Bitcoin was extended to contract execution between two or more parties in a fully decentralized manner.

Bitcoin's potential value is far larger than what is assumed. In Marc Andreessen's words, "Bitcoin is a classic network effect, a positive feedback loop. The more people who use bitcoin, the more valuable bitcoin is for everyone who uses it, and the higher the incentive for the next user to start using the technology" (Andreessen, 2014).

WHAT IS BITCOIN: WALL STREET VIEW

Investors want to classify their investments into various asset classes. Asset allocation is an essential aspect of portfolio construction and management.

An asset class is a group of assets with common economic and governance factors affecting their prices. For example, US large-cap stocks and emerging markets stocks can be two different asset classes. The US large-cap stocks are the stocks of large US companies whose stock price is dependent on the growth of the US economy and the policy choices of the US government. The emerging market stocks are the stocks of fast-growing developing economies such as India and China, and they are dependent on the economic growth and policies of their respective governments. The two asset classes should have low interrelationships and act as separate asset classes from investing perspectives.

Bitcoin is a new type of investment, as it provides an infrastructure for many potential usages. This makes its classification into an asset class difficult. Wall Street is full of debates, often acrimonious, about almost every aspect of bitcoin. These debates usually start when the bitcoin price makes a parabolic move. Such moves have come roughly every four years. These debates reach a crescendo as bitcoin price goes to the moon, like in 2012, 2016, and currently in 2020–2021.

In 2014, Aswath Damodaran, a professor of finance at New York University, wrote, "The reason for the divide, though, is the two sides seem to disagree fundamentally on what bitcoin is, and at the risk of raising hackles all the way around, I will argue bitcoin is not an asset, but a currency, and as such, you cannot value it or invest in it. You can only price it and trade it" (Damodaran, 2017).

According to Damodaran, every investment has to fall into one of these categories: cash-generating assets, commodity, currency, or collectible. A cash-generating asset can be valued by calculating the present value of its future cash flows or comparing it against similar assets whose value is known. Commodities derive their value from their use to meet a fundamental need. Commodities can be valued using their price histories.

A currency has three functions: a unit of account, a medium of exchange, and a store of value. Currencies do not have cash flows and cannot be valued. Currencies can only be priced against other currencies. One currency's relative strength against another depends on how good it is performing the three functions. Collectibles have none of the properties of the other three investments. Collectibles, like a painting or a sculpture, may have an aesthetic value, but they can only be priced based on their desirability and scarcity.

Damodaran argues bitcoin is not an asset because it has no cash flows. Bitcoin is not a commodity since it cannot be used as a raw material in producing something useful. It may be a currency, but its use as a medium of exchange is still limited.

There are significant ramifications to bitcoin potentially being a currency and nothing else. A currency cannot be an asset or used as a portfolio diversifier—an important ingredient of portfolio construction. Currencies in financial markets can only be priced against other currencies and traded as such. According to this school of thought, traders can speculate about the future price of bitcoin and bet accordingly. But this kind of speculation has a negative connotation and does not have a direct place in an investment portfolio.

Damodaran wrote another article in 2017 about bitcoin and other cryptocurrencies, focusing on their function as currency. Damodaran writes, "If you define success as a rise in market capitalization and popular interest, cryptocurrencies have succeeded, perhaps more quickly than its original proponents ever expected them to." Cryptocurrencies' total market capitalization had reached from a mere five billion dollars in 2014 to a whopping 535 billion dollars by December 2017. Whether the success due to price rise was a temporary one or an important milestone in the long-term depended on how bitcoin and other cryptocurrencies performed on three primary functions of a currency.

UNIT OF ACCOUNT

A unit of account allows us to value assets, liabilities, goods, and services. A currency can be a good unit of account if it is fungible and divisible. When you receive your paycheck in dollars and use them to make grocery purchases, the dollars received and paid are identical. This is the fungibility property of a currency. Bitcoin is fungible, and it is divisible up to the eighth place of the decimal.

MEDIUM OF EXCHANGE

A currency is a good medium of exchange if it is easily accessible and transportable and trusted by many buyers and sellers as a legal tender. Bitcoin and other cryptocurrencies are easily accessible and transferable. There is no central authority managing flow of bitcoins, making it a truly disinter-mediated currency. The absence of a central authority makes bitcoins widely accessible. They are also native to the medium in which they are transferred—computer bytes being transferred over computer networks, which makes bitcoin and other digital assets extremely accessible and transportable at a very low or no cost.

STORE OF VALUE

In the short-term, bitcoin prices can fluctuate significantly. However, in the longer term, it has shown a sustainable price rise. The new supply of bitcoins is controlled by computer code. The controlled supply and cap on total bitcoins will lead to low inflation over the longer term. All of this makes bitcoin a good store of value. In the long run, as bitcoin liquidity increases, the prices will become less volatile. **Liquidity generally means how quickly an asset can be bought or sold without affecting its price substantially.**

Central banks around the world have been printing fiat currencies at an unprecedented rate. In Damodaran's words, "The rise of Bitcoin in the last four years has coincided with the *Age of Hubris* in central banking, where central bankers have donned Superman capes and viewed their mission as saving economies rather than protecting their currencies. It is also worth speculating whether money that would have normally flowed to gold, historically the prime beneficiary of loss of trust in central banks, has flowed instead into bitcoin, explaining both the anemic price behavior of the former and the heady price action in the latter."

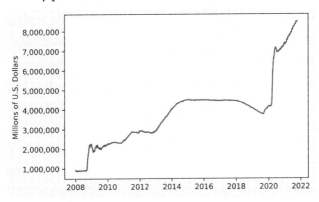

US Federal Reserve Balance Sheet 2008–2021

Bitcoin is a clear beneficiary of loss of trust in the fiat currencies. Bitcoin is decentralized, and its total supply is limited to twenty million coins. In January 2020, there will be about 15.6 million bitcoins in circulation. New coins are regularly generated by a fixed and open-source computer algorithm that is entirely transparent and accessible to everyone.

However, arguments about bitcoin's performance as a currency miss an essential aspect of the underlying technology. We saw in Silicon Valley's view of Bitcoin that **bitcoin and other cryptocurrencies could be useful in many more ways than a fiat currency or gold could be.**

FINDING BITCOIN IN FACEBOOK

The two views of Bitcoin above sound like they are two different things. Wall Street is ignoring the fact bitcoin and other cryptocurrencies are nascent technologies whose value proposition could be significantly transformational while they come of age. On the other hand, Silicon Valley is oblivious to the important considerations of portfolio and risk management fundamental to Wall Street's approach to analyzing and managing liquid instruments. A liquid instrument is an asset that can be easily bought and sold for cash.

Investors on both sides of the debate are perturbed by the hybrid nature of Bitcoin. It is like a VC-backed start-up but traded like stocks and currencies. Such difficulty was never faced by Facebook during its start-up journey, as VCs backed it until it started trading publicly on stock exchanges, where it moved from VCs to Wall Street. Bitcoin, on the other hand, was public on day one. A start-up that trades on public exchanges becomes accessible to everyone.

A start-up has a completely different risk-and-reward profile compared to a publicly traded stock of a large company like Facebook. This is why a different type of investor—the VCs—were invested in Facebook, the start-up, vs. Facebook, the publicly traded company, whose stock is bought and sold by a broad swathe of investors, including individuals and institutions trading on Wall Street.

Bitcoin is a new technology as well as a traded instrument. Contrast this with Facebook, the company, and Facebook, the stock. The tools of analysis and investment used by the VCs and Wall Street are juxtaposed in cryptocurrencies.

In the next several chapters, you will learn how to analyze early-stage technology companies' value drivers. Fundamental to such analysis is an understanding of how similar technologies have grown in the past. When you are dealing with new technology like blockchain, you do not have historical data to predict how it will evolve. In such a scenario, you can learn from similar past technologies.

Public blockchain technologies, such as Bitcoin and Ethereum, are in many ways a progression of the Internet, which makes the Internet an ideal technology to learn from.

After you have learned the VC way of analyzing the cryptocurrencies in Sections Two and Three, you will move to the Wall Street way of building a portfolio of these assets in Sections Four and Five.

CHAPTER 3

A Brave New World

———

*"The Web reminds me of the early days of the PC industry.
No one really knows anything. All experts have been wrong."*

—STEVE JOBS

If you look at the growth of Bitcoin and other cryptocurrency protocols over the past decades, you could say no one knows anything about cryptocurrencies and all experts will be proven wrong.

We see the same story get repeated with cryptocurrencies because they are a foundational technology, very much like the Internet. **It is difficult to predict the growth of foundational technologies because they work at a far deeper level of the economic systems in bringing change than what a typical analyst is accustomed to.**

We will look at the development of the Internet to understand how a foundational technology takes shape. This exercise is also important because the blockchain protocols are running on top of the Internet. This gives rise to the idea of Web 3.0, where a large number of disruptive products are getting built.

A GALE CREATIVE DESTRUCTION

According to Mark J. Perry, a senior fellow at The American Enterprise Institute, "only fifty-two US companies have been on the Fortune 500 list since 1955 when it was first released." The gale of creative destruction brought about by innovation and technological change has reshaped business and economies unpredictably.

There are forty-three Internet computer software and information technology companies on the Fortune 500 that did not exist in 1955. The top seven of the world's ten largest companies by market capitalization are Internet and software companies. None of them, except for Microsoft, were in the top ten in 2000, and the Internet and software did not exist in 1955.

The creative destruction, where the old world gave way to the new world of business, was brought about by two major technological advancements: the personal computer (PC) and the Internet. The foundational work on both roughly started in the '50s.

Joseph Schumpeter, an economist, regarded as one of the twentieth century's greatest intellectuals, published his influential work on creative destruction, *Capitalism, Socialism, and Democracy* in 1942. A few years later, Hungarian-born mathematician John von Neumann outlined the architecture of a programmable computer, which became the blueprint of modern computing devices, bringing the third and fourth industrial revolutions.

According to Schumpeter, capitalism thrives by the innovation of entrepreneurs who bring radical ideas to break existing monopolies and oligopolies. These monopolies and oligopolies survive due to high barriers new entrants have to break. To describe this phenomenon, Schumpeter introduced the term "creative destruction" as the force that sustains long-term economic growth while it destroys the value of established companies.

Using Google Scholar, LSE (London School of Economics) Impact Blog ranks Schumpeter's book *Capitalism, Socialism, and Democracy* as the third most cited book in social sciences published before 1950, behind Karl Marx's *Capital* and Adam Smith's *The Wealth of Nations*.

In this book, Joseph Schumpeter said:

"The opening up of new markets and the organizational development from the craft shop and factory to such concerns as US Steel illustrate the process of industrial mutation that incessantly revolutionizes the economic structure from within, incessantly destroying the old one, incessantly creating a new one... [The process] must be seen in its role in the perennial gale of creative destruction; it cannot be understood on the hypothesis there is a perennial lull" (Schumpeter, 1962).

Bitcoin did not exist before 2009. Its current market capitalization will make it the fifth-largest company in the United States after Microsoft, Apple, Amazon, and Alphabet (Google). The blockchain technology behind cryptocurrencies can be seen as the driving mutation that will revolutionize the modern economic structures from within.

FOUNDATIONAL TECHNOLOGY

Blockchain, which is the technology behind Bitcoin, was listed as one of the top ten emerging technologies for 2016 by experts at the World Economic Forum.

Foundational technology like the Internet, railroad, telegraph, and electricity can change how the world works at the socioeconomic level. Foundational technologies don't arrive overnight. They are often built upon decades of scientific, engineering, and infrastructure development that move in an unpredictable manner (Iansiti, 2017). Only by looking in hindsight can one connect the dots and create a story about how we arrived at the present.

The first transatlantic cables were successfully laid in 1857, giving birth to the analog communications technology, the telegraph. In 1942, John von Neumann laid the blueprint of computers. In 1948, Claude Shannon developed the mathematical principles behind digital communications.

The Internet was kickstarted in 1994 by the launch of the Netscape browser, but with the arrival of the iPhone in 2007, more than a billion people could hold the power of the Internet in their hands.

To understand how a foundational technology shapes our socioeconomic world's contours, we will delve deeper into how the Internet came to be.

INTERNET: A FOUNDATIONAL TECHNOLOGY

In the beginning, the Internet grew slowly. The fundamental building blocks took decades to develop.

On October 4, 1957, the Soviets sent an object in space—Sputnik 1, the first artificial Earth satellite. Soviet success came as a shock to the United States and started a new era of an arms race in outer space, leading to unprecedented technological and scientific development. The United States and the rest of the western world saw the Soviet success in sending an object to space as a threat. The Soviets could use the same technology to drop nuclear bombs anywhere in the world.

The Sputnik crisis shook America's confidence in its scientific and technical capabilities. In response, President Dwight D. Eisenhower established the Advanced Research Projects Agency (ARPA), which was responsible for the development of emerging technologies for the US military to counter perceived Soviet superiority in researching and developing military technology.

ARPA became the US government's top research body tasked with high-risk, high-gain, far-out fundamental research. The boldness of these objectives attracted the nation's leading scientists and engineers to ARPA. These brilliant minds developed America's first successful satellite in a record eighteen months.

ARPA started with space research and later played an early role in Transit, the predecessor of the Global Positioning Systems (GPS). In 1962, Dr. J. C. R. Licklider became head of ARPA's research with a mission to develop military-use computer technology.

Licklider, a visionary in computer networking, had a mandate to connect the US Department of Defense's computers around the United States. As a nuclear war with the USSR absorbed Americans' imaginations, the military needed a reliable system to remotely manage its assets across the United States in case of a nuclear attack when supposedly most of the infrastructure would crumble under the nuclear dust.

Licklider also had a less urgent yet important objective to create a collaborative environment for top scientists around the United States. He saw an interactive use of computers as a tool to create a critical mass of intellectual resources.

In the 1960s, ARPA researchers, in collaboration with researchers around the United States, set out to solve many problems with connecting separate physical networks in a single, whole, logical network. One of the major problems in establishing such connectivity related to the message switching systems the early networks used. This system required a rigid routing protocol, which used a dedicated line between two communicating nodes (computers). This system had a single point of failure—if the link between the two communicating entities was broken, they would fail to communicate.

The problem with message switching led to the development of packet switching. In packet switching, a message will be broken into multiple packets at the host and will opportunistically travel through a network of links until they reach the recipient, where they will be extracted and combined together. In this approach, if a packet found a broken link on its path, it would divert to a nearby healthy link, which moved the packet forward toward its target. Packet switching led to better bandwidth utilization, faster response times, and a fault-tolerant system of communication that was a major breakthrough in development in wide area networks (WAN) that connected a larger geographical region into a single interconnected network.

According to Gregory Gromov's "Roads and Crossroads of the Internet History," at 22:30 hours on October 29, 1969, the first link was established between the University of California, Los Angeles (UCLA) and the Stanford Research Institute (SRI) in what would become known as ARPANET. Leonard Kleinrock, a top researcher, and his graduate students at UCLA hoped to log onto the SRI computer and send it some data remotely. They planned to type "login" and confirm via phone call if the message was received on the far-off SRI computer.

Kleinrock said in an interview:

"We typed the L, and we asked on the phone,

"Do you see the L?"

"Yes, we see the L," came the response.

"We typed the O," and we asked, "Do you see the O?"

"Yes, we see the O."

"Then we typed the G, and the system crashed...

"Yet a revolution had begun..."

(Gromov, 2012).

The Internet was born.

By December 1969, the University of Utah and University of California, Santa Barbara were also added, turning ARPANET into a four-node network. Around the same time, many networks were successfully created at various universities across the United States. Scientists at the University of Hawai'i at Mānoa transmitted data to seven computers on four islands in Hawaii.

As several independent networks using a disparate set of technologies and architecture sprang up at research institutions across the United States, it became clear a core system and set of rules and processes were needed for these disparate networks to communicate with each other. Transmission Control Protocol (TCP) and Internet Protocol (IP) were born. The TCP/IP protocol added a layer on top of the existing networks that allowed them to interact with each other even though each of them transmitted information differently.

You can think of the TCP/IP protocol as a layer through which different underlying networks can communicate.

TCP/IP made the network connection between different networks hardware agnostic and led to the fast growth of networks and the internetwork, now known as the Internet. These internetworks grew and, in turn, gave further rise to collaboration, exchange of data, and access to remote computing resources to the researchers and academicians across continents. ARPANET became the technical core and backbone of the system that would become the Internet.

During the '80s, the Internet continued to bring more collaboration between researchers from government and academic institutions, making Licklider's vision a reality. The primary application of the Internet remained email, file sharing, gaming, and remote access to computer resources.

BIRTH OF WEB AS A BY-PRODUCT OF PHYSICS EXPERIMENTS

In the early '80s, CERN, the European Organization for Nuclear Research, adopted the TCP/IP protocol. At the time, CERN was the world's largest research laboratory, with thousands of physicists and engineers around the world participating in research of high energy physics. The community at CERN generated an enormous amount of data strewn across the laboratory's computers and storage. People often needed to access a particular computer to get the data from it. The method of finding data was quite inefficient.

In 1990, Tim Berners-Lee, a scientist at CERN, proposed a model for the World Wide Web which would provide an interface allowing people to search through the information available on a computer network and present it to the user on a computer terminal. This interface—Web—used hypertext, "a way to link and access information of various kinds as a web of nodes in which the user can browse at will. It provides a single-user interface to large classes of information (reports, notes, databases, computer documentation, and online help)," (Gromov, 2012).

The information on the network could be text, image, or speech and would be indexed and searchable by any computer with the World Wide Web software program. This was a revolutionary idea, as it would allow the researchers quick access to a piece of specific information from an enormous and exponentially growing amount of data distributed on computers around the world. With the introduction of the World Wide Web, CERN became the largest Internet site in Europe and influenced the acceptance and spread of the Internet worldwide.

The browser was released to the general public in 1991. At the same time, the US government decommissioned ARPANET, and the Internet was opened to the world. Netscape Navigator, written by Marc Andreessen, was released in December 1994, providing the first commercial Web browser. The Netscape browser spread like wildfire, making the Internet a household name and bringing the dot-com boom.

A BOOM OF CREATIVE BUST

Over the next few years, many Internet start-ups were started, including Amazon, Netflix, Webvan, America Online, Netflix, and Google.

Many would bite the dust when the bubble exploded in 2000, but others like Amazon, Google, and Netflix would go on to disrupt the incumbents in their industries. They created a vast amount of wealth and value for their investors and users through the creative destruction that changed how the world worked.

The dot-com bust was followed by a bubble in telecom when telecom equipment companies would spend more than five hundred billion dollars to lay fiber optic cables and build wireless networks, giving rise to the modern era of the Internet in which more than three billion people access the Internet with handheld devices.

The boom and bust cycle led to growth in infrastructure that would not have been possible without a bubble.

As complementary technologies like telecommunication and microprocessors grew, the Internet became a huge wealth generator. Starting as a military project and closed to the world until 1991, the Internet has redefined society, politics, and the economy.

Fred Wilson, a highly successful venture capitalist who founded several Internet companies and lost more than 90 percent of his investment in the dot-com bust, said:

"A friend of mine has a great line. He says, 'Nothing important has ever been built without irrational exuberance,' meaning you need some of this mania to cause investors to open up their pocketbooks and finance the building of the railroads or the automobile or aerospace industry or whatever. In this case, much of the capital invested was lost, but also much of it was invested in a very high throughput backbone for the Internet, and lots of software that works, and databases and server structure. All that stuff has allowed what we have today, which has changed all our lives... That's what all this speculative mania built" (Quinn et al. 2020).

LONG LIVE THE INTERNET

The Internet was built on the need to share data in a speedy and decentralized manner over the wires. It took decades of research and development, from the time when researchers in Santa Barbara sent three letters to a computer in Stanford using technologies that would create the backbone of the Internet to the modern-day when most of the world can create and share high-definition content from their mobile devices.

Bitcoin protocol allows value to be transferred over the networks without a central entity. This concept is analogous to the Internet, which transfers data over the networks in a decentralized manner.

Blockchain is a foundational technology built on top of the Internet. Many of the Internet era players are active in the blockchain space, making it a speedier journey because a lot of knowledge learned in the Internet's development is getting reapplied to the development of public blockchain technologies and networks, such as Bitcoin and Ethereum.

PART 2

THE TECHIE

Blockchain and cryptocurrency are a revolution in finance brought about by decades of innovation in cryptography and digital cash. In this section, you will gain a deeper understanding of the key innovations behind blockchain and cryptocurrencies.

By the end of this section, you will learn:

- How a battle cry for privacy in the online world developed many core components of Bitcoin technology.

- What Bitcoin, a fully decentralized peer-to-peer electronic payment system, is.

- How the core ideas behind Bitcoin gave rise to the execution of smart contracts on the decentralized world computers.

- How smart contracts lead to the development of decentralized applications (dApps).

CHAPTER 4

The Crypto Anarchy
of Cypherpunks

———

"If privacy is outlawed, only outlaws will have privacy."

—PHIL ZIMMERMANN

You can give someone cash and never worry about it again. You send someone money on the Internet and the transaction is recorded until the end of the time.

Eric Hughes, a privacy activist, wrote in an essay titled "A Cypherpunk's Manifesto":

"A private matter is something one doesn't want the whole world to know, but a secret matter is something one doesn't want anybody to know. Privacy is the power to selectively reveal oneself to the world."

As the Internet grew from an email system in 1969 on the ARPANET to the World Wide Web in the 1990s, privacy concerns took center stage. Many security professionals and academicians worried the Internet would not protect the freedom and privacy people took for granted in the offline world. The nefarious actors could see Internet data flowing through the communication channels.

The only way to protect the privacy of citizens, cryptography, was under government control. A movement driven by mathematicians and computer scientists was born in the 1970s to free cryptography and the Internet from the prying eyes of governments. The stakes were high—the Internet would log every message and transaction. If they were not secured with cryptography, it would bring a dystopia of Orwellian proportions, where Big Brother will watch every action on the Internet.

The movement gave birth to the cypherpunks, who waged and won a war with the US government in the early '90s over use of cryptography. The freedom of cryptography for public use will herald an era of prosperity on the Internet and will culminate with the invention of a peer-to-peer electronic cash, the bitcoin. In the end, cypherpunks would free both money and speech on the Internet.

This chapter will go on a journey with cypherpunks and discover core components of Bitcoin, just like they did.

THE FIRST "PUBLIC" CRYPTOGRAPHY

Using cryptography, a sender can "encrypt" a message by using a key to hide its content, so it appears as a random string of numbers and characters. The receiver can then "decrypt" the message by using a key to recreate the original message.

There are two primary methods to achieve encryption. In a symmetric key cryptography, the same key is used to encrypt and decrypt the message. When symmetric key encryption is used, the message is encrypted to look garbled to the intruder, but the key must also be sent over this channel. If the intruder intercepts the key, then he can use the key to decrypt any following messages that were encrypted using it. In an asymmetric key cryptography, a different key is used for encryption and decryption, and the sender does not send his encryption key to the receiver.

For example, in a simple symmetric key cryptography scheme, we can create an encrypted message by swapping each letter with the following letter in the alphabet.

Suppose, in World War II, the headquarters of Allied forces asked their ground troops to attack Normandy Beach.

Plaintext Message: ATTACK NORMANDY IN MORNING

Cyphertext Message: BUUBDL OPSNBOEZ JO NPSOJOH

The Allied troops near Normandy will receive the cyphertext and the key, "create an encrypted message by swapping each letter with the following letter in the alphabet," and use this key in reverse to convert the cyphertext back to plain text.

In modern times, cryptography has become far more powerful, and it has been used to encrypt and secure messages sent by spies, diplomats, and governments. During World War II, the United Kingdom created a center at Bletchley Park, which became the code-breaking center for the Allied forces. To crack German cyphers, the Allied forces took help from mathematicians such as Alan Turing, the father of theoretical computer science and artificial intelligence.

To control research, development, and use of cryptography, the United States government created the National Security Agency (NSA) in 1952, formed from a unit that deciphered coded communications of the enemy during World War II.

Until the mid-'90s, strong cryptography was controlled by the NSA and put on the US Munitions List, making it unlawful to export strong cryptography along with tankers and bombers. It is not difficult to see why the government wanted to keep cryptography on the export control list. If instructions to the troops on the ground could not be sent securely, it would be difficult to execute surprise attacks across enemy lines.

The NSA continued to control any research on cryptography until 1975, when math whiz Whitfield Diffie and his collaborator, Martin Hellman, both at the computer science department at Stanford, published a paper on public-key cryptography.

DIFFIE-HELMAN AND DEMOCRATIZATION OF ONLINE SECURITY

Whitfield Diffie developed an interest in cryptography at an early age. In computing historian Steven Levy's July 1994 *New York Times Magazine* article, it says, "He had been bitten by the cryptography bug at age ten when his father, a professor, brought home the entire crypto shelf of the City College Library in New York."

Diffie later went to the Massachusetts Institute of Technology (MIT) to pursue a major in mathematics. Once at MIT, he became worried about the security and privacy of data secured on computer hard drives and disks. At the time, the user data such as emails and files were secured using a password. All the user passwords were saved in a file or a database controlled by a system administrator. To Diffie, this system had a flaw, as the user's privacy was in the hands of another human being—the system administrator. Users of the computer system would have put their research, identifying information, and even intimate secrets in the system administrator's hands. According to Levy, Diffie worried,

"You may have protected files, but if a subpoena were served to the system manager, it wouldn't do you any good. The administrators would sell you out because they'd have no interest in going to jail."

In the early 1970s, researchers at ARPANET, the Internet's predecessor, were looking to identify security options to secure communication between its members. At the time, NSA's encryption technology, called DES, used a symmetric key encryption.

As we saw in the previous section, in the symmetric key cryptography, the key needs to be shared between the sender and receiver of an encrypted message. The problem multiplies when a large number of people use the communication channel, such as on the Internet. In such a scenario, many keys will need to be saved in digital vaults administered by an administrator, creating a single point of failure. The situation is similar to one described above, with the system administrator at MIT having access to the file containing passwords of all users and the ability to peek into the users' private lives. In such a setting, to access every users' information on the Internet, an intruder would need to attack a single place, the digital vault of the keys, making it a single point of failure.

Diffie took it upon himself to solve this problem. In 1975, Diffie and his collaborator, Martin Hellman, published the public-key cryptography scheme. In public-key cryptography, a pair of keys are used instead of a single key in a symmetric scheme described above. Public-key cryptography is an asymmetric key scheme. In public-key cryptography, a password-like private key—a random string of numbers and characters—is used to generate a public key for each user. The method to generate a public key from a private key provides mathematical guarantees that no one can guess the private key even if everyone knows the public key.

Let's take an example using fictional characters Alice and Bob to understand the Public-key cryptography scheme. Using this scheme, if Alice wanted to send a message to Bob securely, Alice would use Bob's public key to encrypt the message. This message can only be decrypted using Bob's private key. Once Bob receives the message, he will use his private key to decrypt the message. No private keys are exchanged over the communication channel. Since only Bob has his private key, only he can decrypt the message.

An additional advantage of this scheme is Alice could digitally sign a document or message using her private key and send the document to Bob. Bob uses Alice's public key to validate her signature, ensuring the message came from Alice and was not tampered with while in transit. This is guaranteed because if an intruder wanted to change the message in transit, he would have to use his private key to sign the modified message. Since the intruder's private key did not generate Alice's public key, Bob would not be able to decrypt the message using her key, raising a red flag.

This work will later lead to the solution of two major problems of cryptography—(1) how to send encrypted messages over insecure channels without needing a third party to secure the encryption (private) keys and (2) how to sign and authenticate messages and documents digitally. Above all, this was a decentralized system where no central digital vault of keys existed under the prying eyes of a system administrator or the government.

The scheme was created outside the US government and available to the general public. It turned out this scheme was superior to the Data Encryption Standard (DES) the government and NSA had approved for common use. DES was developed at an IBM Research lab and suffered from the rumors the government had created a backdoor, which the NSA denied (Levy, 1994).

The Diffie-Hellman scheme was soon implemented by three MIT scientists—Ron Rivest, Adi Shamir, and Leonard Adleman. The algorithm came to be known as RSA, which was patented by MIT and licensed to RSA Data Security, a firm building privacy and authentication tools.

E-CASH

Diffie-Hellman's paper and RSA algorithm encouraged privacy-focused researchers to push the boundaries of privacy on the Internet. These advocates imagined a day when the Internet would not only be used for file exchange and gaming but also become a virtual marketplace where e-commerce would thrive. They felt a need for electronic cash which would provide the same privacy guarantees as real cash.

Think for a moment about how a cash transaction is different from an online transaction using your debit card.

CASH TRANSACTION

Alice and Bob meet in person and exchange goods for cash.

ONLINE TRANSACTION

Alice and Bob meet online. Alice uses her debit card to buy goods from Bob.

Alice's bank authenticates her identity. Using its ledger, Alice's bank makes sure she has sufficient balance in her account. Alice's bank blocks the amount, usually more than requested, to ensure Alice does not spend the same money in another transaction while the bank is going through the tedious process of authentication, validation, and confirmation.

Alice's bank sends a message to Bob's bank saying money is being sent to an account number that is (hopefully) associated with Bob's account.

Bob's bank validates his account on its ledger.

Both banks settle the transaction through a central ledger held by the central bank. Alice's bank debits the amount from her account on its ledger. Bob's bank credits the amount to his account on its ledger.

From a privacy perspective, every transaction Alice or Bob do online gets recorded in various places. Both are at the mercy of their banks to complete the transaction. To handle the complexity of this transaction, banks also need to create costly infrastructure for security, compliance, data recording, auditing, and reporting. This cost is often passed on to the bank customers. Banks hold the ledger, giving them control over individuals' money.

The solution is to create digital cash. It should provide the same privacy guarantees as real cash without a third party, such as a bank in the above example.

However, creating something of value on the Internet without using a trusted third party no one can copy and reuse is extremely difficult. As we go through the journey that will take us to create the first decentralized electronic cash system, Bitcoin, you will discover how difficult it is.

THE CRYPTO WARS

The Diffie-Hellman scheme was implemented by the MIT trio and patented by RSA Data Security. Even though the algorithm was developed outside the government, the NSA continued to push for keeping strong cryptography for government use only. Many in the cryptography community did not believe RSA Data Security would push back against government pressure and not open a backdoor to allow the government to listen into the online communications.

The control of the RSA algorithm by RSA Data Security, a private company, incensed another activist—Phil Zimmermann.

Phil set out to implement the RSA algorithm. Working on the algorithm for several years while missing five mortgage payments, Phil finally completed his encryption software in 1991. The software was named PGP for "Pretty Good Privacy." Phil told Steven Levy, "I came within an inch of losing my house" (Levy, 1994).

Phil released PGP as free software, which was quickly downloaded around the world. PGP was the first publicly available strong encryption software, now used by email programs around the world.

"You may be planning a political campaign, discussing your taxes, or having an illicit affair. Or you may be doing something you feel shouldn't be illegal but is. Whatever it is, you don't want your private electronic mail or confidential documents read by anyone else. There's nothing wrong with asserting your privacy. Privacy is as apple-pie as the Constitution," wrote Zimmermann in his 1994 essay.

Meanwhile, a battle was brewing between the NSA and privacy-focused cryptography researchers.

CLIPPER CHIP

In 1993, the Clinton administration supported an NSA proposal, which requires telecommunications companies to include a chipset known as the Clipper chip. Clipper chip was an encryption device to secure voice and data messages flowing through the phone lines, but with a built-in backdoor that would allow government agencies to decode intercepted communications.

The proposal generated an immediate backlash from the Electronic Frontier Foundation, Electronic Privacy Information Center, privacy advocates, academics, and many members of Congress, including then-senators John Ashcroft and John Kerry. The opponents argued the backdoor would allow government agencies to do a Big Brother-type of mass surveillance while allowing terrorists, adversarial governments, and state actors to use the same backdoor to gain access to personal communications and data such as medical information and credit ratings.

CYPHERPUNKS ESTABLISHED

A meeting was held in late 1992 in San Francisco Bay Area by Eric Hughes, a brilliant Berkeley mathematician; Tim May, a former chief scientist at Intel who, through his stock options, had retired at the age of thirty-four; and John Gilmore, a wealthy computer scientist who was number five at the Sun Microsystems and cofounder of Electronic Frontier Foundation, an organization to advocate cyberspace freedom.

The group was informal and included activists, cryptographers, and mathematicians driven by the common cause of privacy in telecommunications. They were worried the Internet would soon penetrate commercial and social spheres of life and the world was not prepared to protect its privacy from government surveillance.

The group was jokingly called "cypherpunks" by one of its participants, Judith Milton, who was known by the pseudonym "St. Jude." The name was derived from "cypher" and "cyberpunk," a subgenre of science fiction focusing on dystopian futuristic settings and high tech.

The group created a mailing list open to anyone interested in discussions on a range of topics, including technology, privacy, and politics. They used Phil Zimmermann's PGP software to encrypt their conversation, which allowed the free flow of ideas. The list allowed users outside the Bay Area to become part of the group, and the number of users quickly grew to over seven hundred in the next five years.

REMAILER ATTACKS

To ensure privacy of their communications and government sensitivity around cryptography, the cypherpunk mail list used remailers. A remailer is a software that forwards emails anonymously. A user sends an email to the common remailer address, then the remailer anonymizes the sender and forwards the email to all members on its list. This worked perfectly for cypherpunks, as they could freely discuss their ideas without worrying someone might try to link their messages back to their real identities.

The remailers had a flaw, though—it could be used to spam the inboxes of everyone on the list. Spam messages are very cheap to generate, as the spammer can use a bot to create and send millions of copies of an email. A spammer can bombard a remailer, which will then flood the mailboxes of its members. On the other hand, members won't be able to use the remailer, as it would be busy forwarding messages from the spammer. This is also called a denial-of-service (DoS) attack.

ADAM BACK: PROOF OF WORK (POW) (1997)

Adam Back, a cypherpunk and a computer scientist, proposed a solution to the remailer problem. In Back's solution, a very small cost was introduced into the remailer server that becomes prohibitively expensive when multiplied for a large number of requests, such as a spam attack.

A server is a computer program that serves clients with data when requested. For example, your web browser is a client which you use to open a website, then send a request to the server operated by that website, which is also known as a web server. For example, you send a search request using Google's website in a chrome browser to a server operated by Google, which responds with an answer to your search queries.

The algorithm was called hashcash. In the hashcash algorithm, when an email is sent, the sender computer is expected to solve a puzzle called **hash** that takes a small amount of computing (CPU) resources. The sender includes the puzzle solution into the email header as proof of work. You can think of this solution as a postage stamp or cash because computing resources were spent in creating this hash. Adam Back wrote on the cypherpunk mailing list, **"The idea of using... hashes is they can be made arbitrarily expensive to compute... and yet can be verified instantly."** When the email server of a recipient receives this email, including the hash, the recipient email server looks at the header first and validates the hash solution before accepting the full body of the email. This proof of work is negligible in the case of regular emails because a sender is expected to send only a limited number of emails in its lifetime, but it can exponentially rise when done for billions of emails, as in the case of a spammer, making it uneconomic for the spammer to send those emails.

However, there was a difficulty with this approach. A hash, once calculated, could be used multiple times. To solve this problem, Adam proposed the calculated hashes could be saved in a central database so a hash will only be accepted if it is absent in the database, validating the originality of the hash—that is, it has never been seen before.

Nowadays, a different type of proof of work is often included in many web pages to control the denial-of-service (DoS) attacks. When entering such web pages, you may need to solve an image puzzle or write a CAPTCHA before you are allowed entry. The image puzzles and CAPTCHA are easy for humans to read and solve but difficult for the bots, making it uneconomical for bots to attack the web server of these websites.

Even though hashcash was created to solve a problem unrelated to digital currency, proof of work will become a fundamental building block of digital cash experiments. It will form the basis of techniques to achieve decentralization in Bitcoin and other cryptocurrency protocols.

WEI DAI: B-MONEY (1998)

Wei Dai, a computer scientist from the University of Washington, took Adam Back's idea of digital minting of hashcash and proposed a pseudonymous and distributed electronic cash network called b-money.

In Dai's electronic cash system, the identities on the network will be created by using public-key cryptography, and the participants will remain pseudonymous.

In Dai's b-money protocol, anyone can create or "mine" b-money using computational work by solving a previously unsolved computational puzzle and broadcasting the message to a network of computers, which will validate the solution. The computers on the network will use a collective database ledger to keep individuals' accounts and update them as new money is minted by the protocol's participants and exchanged between them. The servers will be rewarded for their work by earning b-money.

In describing the creation of b-money, Dai wrote, "The only conditions are it must be easy to determine how much computing effort it took to solve the problem and the solution must otherwise have no value, either practical or intellectual. The number of monetary units created is equal to the cost of the computing effort in terms of the standard basket of commodities."

The consensus on the state of the accounts and execution of contracts was achieved through a majority voting by the computer servers participating in the network. To keep these servers honest, "each server [was] required to deposit a certain amount of money in a special account to be used as potential fines or rewards for proof of misconduct," wrote Dai. Participating servers were required to stake their money to have a vote in the system. This concept, which will become known as **proof of stake (POS)**, will be later used by Ethereum and many other blockchain protocols. Remember from Chapter 2 that proof of work (POW) used in Bitcoin protocol consumes a large amount of energy as nodes solve a computationally challenging problem using computing resources that require electricity. Proof of stake does not have such an energy dependence.

Dai's proposal introduced decentralization in the pseudony-mous electronic cash system. However, the proposal did not provide a complete practical design for the implementation, and his ideas were not implemented.

The b-money system proposal first imagined a method to create value on the Internet which could be safely exchanged between various participants in its network without relying on any single one of them or a trusted third party to ensure honesty in the system. These ideas will become the core prin-ciples used behind the creation of Bitcoin.

CHAPTER 5

Bitcoin: The Internet Money

"We have proposed a system for electronic transactions without relying on trust."

—SATOSHI NAKAMOTO

THE VISION OF SATOSHI

On the eve of Halloween, October 31, 2008, at 2:10 p.m. Eastern Time, an email titled "Bitcoin P2P e-cash paper" was sent to a mail group, metzdowd.com. A group of cryptography enthusiasts managed this mail group. Satoshi Nakamoto, the pseudonymous author of the email, wrote, "I've been working on a new electronic cash system that's fully peer-to-peer, with no trusted third party."

Nine pages long, the whitepaper promised to disintermediate the global financial payment system run by a network of large financial institutions such as JPMorgan Chase and Bank of America and payment processors like Visa and Mastercard.

Satoshi started the article by writing, "A peer-to-peer version of electronic cash would allow online payments to be sent directly from one party to another without going through a financial institution" (Nakamoto, 2008).

The publication of the whitepaper could not be timelier. In the past two decades, the trust in the central bank, government, and financial institutions had become an embodiment of the American motto *"In God We Trust,"* also printed on many coins and dollar bills. But that trust was shaken to its core due to the ongoing financial crisis of 2007–2008, whose seeds were sown back in early 2000s in the lax lending standard of the financial industry behind subprime mortgages to the borrowers with no ability to pay back their loans. In many cases, these housing loans were given to borrowers without any proof of income—the no-doc loans. As these borrowers started to default on their loans, a cascading fall of mortgage related financial companies took place.

THE GREAT FINANCIAL CRISIS

In the previous month, the developed world was in the throes of the great financial crisis epitomized by the fall of Lehman Brothers, the New York based investment bank, which announced bankruptcy on September 14, 2008. The global financial system was brought to the brink as one institution fell after another like dominoes. By the end of October, many institutions of the twentieth-century financial industry, such as Bear Stearns, Lehman Brothers, and Washington Mutual, vanished in thin air.

Stock markets worldwide had been decimated, taking away people's lifetime of pensions and investments. Toward the end of October, S&P 500 fell by more than 27.2 percent for the month, exceeding not only the Black Monday stock market crash of October 1987 but also coming second to the worst ever percentage decline at the beginning of the Great Depression in September 1931, when S&P 500 lost 29.94 percent.

Alan Greenspan, the former federal chairman who had resided at the top of the US central bank for close to nineteen years and served five terms under four US presidents, admitted before a congressional committee, "Self-regulation by Wall Street had failed. Those of us who looked to the self-interest of lending institutions to protect shareholder's equity—myself especially—are in a state of shocked disbelief (US Government Printing Office, 2008)."

The trust in the Godlike ability of the government, central banks, and financial industry to ensure soundness and security of the financial system and the economy was shattered.

On January 9, 2009, Satoshi Nakamoto, a pseudonym of a group or an individual whose identity remains unknown, released the first version of the Bitcoin software on an open-source software repository, SourceForge. This release launched the Bitcoin network when Satoshi created the first block of the Bitcoin blockchain known as the genesis block (block number zero). The genesis block had a reward of fifty bitcoins, and embedded in this transaction was the text, "*The Times* 03/Jan/2009 Chancellor on the brink of second bailout for banks," referencing a headline published on that day in the UK's *The Times*.

The cryptographer's mail group Satoshi posted to include many cypherpunks, such as Adam Back, Hal Finney, and Nick Szabo, each of whom were thought to be Satoshi Nakamoto. It may never be known who the Bitcoin creator was, but it is clear the electronic cash system Satoshi created was the culmination of over two decades of work by cypherpunks.

In the rest of this chapter, we will delve deeper into the technology behind Bitcoin.

This discussion is presented in an accessible manner to a nontechnical person. You, as an investor, need to have basic knowledge of various terms and processes used in a blockchain protocol. This knowledge will help you understand new products and technologies springing up in the blockchain space.

In order to demonstrate the key concepts and terminology using examples more familiar to readers, I'll first look at how traditional banks work.

HOW DOES A BANK DO WHAT IT DOES

Banks and the financial system sit at the heart of the modern economy. In addition to supporting borrowing and lending, they also allow people and businesses big and small to save and exchange value. They also help create and market contracts that have insurance-like features and support risk-taking in the economy, which is fundamental to growth. Banks are closed, trusted, and centralized institutions that have been around for hundreds of years.

When it comes to processing a payment, banks provide four core services: account identity management, transactions, record management, and trust.

Each bank customer, be it an individual, group, business, or other entity, is assigned an identity and account. The bank asks for identification details and authenticates the customer before any transaction can take place. The customers can receive and send money using bank accounts. If one of the parties to a transaction has an account with a different bank, these banks get involved and make sure the transaction goes through.

Banks will also ensure the party sending money has a sufficient amount in their account and is not sending the same money to multiple parties, a problem known as double-spending. In addition, banks manage records. They internally keep track of all transactions and account balances and provide statements.

Above all, banks provide trust. They are heavily regulated and invest a significant amount of money in developing technology, ensuring the customers' accounts and assets are safe and only valid transactions go through.

To be able to use a bank's services, you need to open an account with that bank—that is, ask their permission to join their system. Banks act as the central party that authenticates identity, validates transactions, and keeps records of transactions and account balances. Every customer of the bank has to trust it to do its job correctly. The customers' transaction history stays with the bank, potentially exposing it to others.

Banks are permissioned, centralized, and trusted systems.

If a new system takes away the trusted central party, then it has to be resilient against malicious and dishonest actors while providing all the services the trusted centralized party provides.

HOW BITCOIN DOES WHAT IT DOES

If a system wants to provide the same services as a bank, it needs to support the following four core services: account and identity management, money transfer as a service, record management, and trust.

Your identity in a value transfer context provides means for authentication so the account associated with that identity can receive money, spend that money, and catch any malicious actor who tries to spend your money.

Additionally, the identity management process should ensure the integrity of the system. For example, when you sign a check, the integrity of the process should ensure no one else can intercept, duplicate, or manipulate your check, meaning the check is tamper-evident.

The concept of identity is ubiquitous in our daily lives. People have public email addresses and private passwords. Houses have public mailboxes and private keys. You give the public part of your identity to others and use the private part to access the items sent to the public part. People can send emails to your public email address, which you can read using your password. This two-part relationship between a public and a private component gives you your identity. Remember how the idea of public address and private password is analogous to the public-key cryptography discussed in Chapter Four. Bitcoin, in fact, uses a public-key cryptography scheme to create identity and secure information on the network.

In Bitcoin, users create their own identities. They pick a private key by randomly generating a sequence of letters and numbers. Then a mathematical function known as a cryptographic hash function is used to take the private key and generate a public key or address. An important property of this mathematical function is no one can guess your private key from your public key or address. Additionally, the chance two private keys will generate the same public address is very low. In fact, the chance of getting hit by a meteorite by the end of this sentence is higher than someone else figuring out your private key from your public address or two private keys generating the same public key.

A bank keeps a central registry of all the identities and makes sure two users don't end up with the same identity. In the case of Bitcoin, that surety is provided by math.

TRANSACTIONS

When a transaction is made in a system, whether a bank or Bitcoin network, it needs to ensure three things:

1. Proof of ownership.

2. Available and sufficient funds.

3. A guarantee no other transaction has used the same funds.

Let's understand this through a transaction via a bank check. When you write a check, you provide your signature, which the bank uses to prove ownership. The bank verifies if you have sufficient funds in your account. As the checks clear in time order, you will not be able to clear checks in amounts larger than the positive balance in your account. If your account goes negative during a transaction, that transaction is rejected as invalid. On the other hand, once a transaction goes through, your account balance is adjusted accordingly.

In the Bitcoin network, there is no central party to keep track of account balances and no central clock to establish the chronological order in which transactions are cleared, making it more complex to manage accounts.

Because the Bitcoin network has no central clock, if you make three transactions sending five bitcoins each from a wallet that has a total of ten bitcoins, it is not clear which two transactions will go through first, as the network is decentralized. Different participants may see these transactions in different orders, leading to a possibility the network validates all three transactions. To reduce this complexity, the Bitcoin network does not use account balances and keeps track of transactions instead. A wallet is a software application that is used to interact with the blockchain ledger and send or receive cryptocurrencies.

Once a transaction is completed in the Bitcoin network—say someone sent you ten bitcoins—a transaction record called unspent transaction output (UTXO) is created. You may have multiple UTXOs coming from different transactions. If you want to spend or send bitcoins to someone else, your UTXOs are added to complete that transaction.

A UTXO can be thought of as a piggy bank. Whenever someone sends you bitcoins, you put them in a piggy bank. When you need to spend or send bitcoins, you start breaking your piggy banks until you have the number of bitcoins you need to send. Any leftover bitcoins from a broken piggy bank are put into a new piggy bank, as you cannot rebuild a shattered piggy bank.

Using UTXOs, it is easier to answer the simpler question, "Does this single piggy bank have enough funds?" instead of asking the more complex question, "Is this account trying to spend more bitcoin than it owns across multiple piggy banks" (Lin et al. 2021)?

RECORD MANAGEMENT

A critical question a system of value exchange needs to answer is who owns what. To answer these questions, banks maintain account balances in their in-house databases.

Different bank departments may maintain customer and balance information in different databases. This gets more complex when transactions involve multiple banks, as each of them has stored information using different formats, software, and hardware. This system is costly due to storage, maintenance, and reconciliation of information across a disparate set of databases across banks.

In the Bitcoin network, the transaction records are stored in a decentralized manner. The database is distributed—all the network participants have equal access with no central entity moderating or managing any aspect of the transaction or recording process. Each node in the network keeps its own copy of the database and updates it when a transaction is broadcast to the network and validated by a majority of nodes.

This type of distribution is also trustless, as each node reads and writes its own copy of the database and does not need to rely on any other node or party to access the transaction history.

In these databases, the transactions are recorded in time-stamped blocks that are appended successively in a chain. The chaining of blocks, where each future block is linked back to the previous blocks, makes this ledger tamper-evident.

Each block is built upon and contains information about the previous. If a node tries to change a transaction in any block of the blockchain (for example, it may try to send bitcoin to itself), all the future blocks become invalidated. This makes this particular copy of blockchain invalid and out of sync with the rest of the network, rendering this malicious change meaningless.

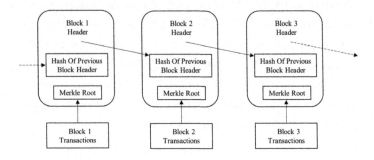

Simplified Blockchain Diagram

CONSENSUS AND TRUST

When everyone has their own copy of the database, how do we make valid updates to the Bitcoin ledger on the network? There is no central place or single source of truth in this ledger. Each node holds its own copy instead.

So, the question is how the ledgers reach consensus on each transaction and remain in sync.

In the Bitcoin ledger, consensus about what transactions to add is reached by majority voting. However, remember the creation of identity is an almost costless process to the Bitcoin network, so we can't have one-identity-one-vote. In such a system where identities can be created in a cost-less manner, a malicious actor can create a large enough number of identities to gain a majority of the votes to change transactions on the Bitcoin network and break the blockchain. This is a similar problem faced by the Cypherpunk remailers, who would be spammed by a large number of emails, as the cost to create an additional copy of emails is zero.

Adam Back developed the hashcash algorithm, which required email senders to provide proof of work for the email server to accept their emails. The work done by legitimate email senders was negligible as the amount of work done per email was low, and the regular senders would send only a limited number of emails in their lifetime. At the same time, this proof of work mechanism made it prohibitively expensive to send a large number of emails to the server to crash it.

On the Bitcoin network, a set of nodes, known as miners, group currently pending transactions into a block and propose that block to the whole network as the next block on the blockchain. The objective of these miners is to collect the transaction fee in the next block and receive newly minted bitcoin for its efforts. As there are many miners that will want to propose a block to the network, there is a competition where each proposer, also known as a miner, competes to solve a computational problem requiring the node to spend computing resources, providing a proof of work. The first node to solve the puzzle gets the right to propose its block to the Bitcoin ledger. In return, it gets the transaction fee and a certain number of new bitcoins that are generated based on the Bitcoin protocol.

Once a miner wins the competition, it proposes its block to the network by broadcasting it to the network participants. The network participants validate the transactions against the history of the transaction on their local copy of the ledger. If a majority of participants validate the transactions in the block, each individual node appends the block to its copy of the blockchain.

The proof of work mechanism ensures if a malicious node or a group of nodes with malicious intent wishes to win the competition, they will have to spend more computing power than the honest nodes. The cost of deploying such computing power is prohibitively expensive in the case of Bitcoin.

The Bitcoin blockchain reaches consensus using proof of work. The blockchain, which is the ledger distributed at each node on the network, remains in sync without any central authority, and a truly decentralized, trustless, and permissionless system is born.

THE NAKAMOTO CONSENSUS

Many of the previous attempts to create an anonymous digital currency for the Internet failed because they depended on a central server to ensure trust.

A partially decentralized system such as the Internet does not go down because even if a part of it does, the information can bypass this part, providing the Internet a high degree of fault tolerance.

The Bitcoin network, like the Internet, provides storage and distribution of information. However, unlike the Internet, **information on the Bitcoin network is saved in a tamper-evident and truly decentralized manner. Your information is not owned by any central entity such as a government or corporation, and you have a right to privacy.** This makes Bitcoin a reliable network for the exchange of value as well as information.

With Bitcoin, cypherpunks achieved the decades-long dream of creating a decentralized electronic cash system. However, that event would be the Big Bang of decentralization everywhere. Using proof of work to arrive at a consensus in a decentralized system will be known as the Nakamoto Consensus, and it will release a genie of decentralization even cypherpunks had not imagined.

CHAPTER 6

Ethereum: The World Computer

———

"Sometimes it is the people no one imagines anything of who do the things no one can imagine."

—ALAN TURING, *THE IMITATION GAME*

A college student gets fascinated by an idea, drops out of college to pursue it, and changes the world. No, I am not talking about Bill Gates or Mark Zuckerberg. I am talking about Vitalik Buterin, a Russian-born Canadian programmer who published the Ethereum whitepaper in 2013, which might disrupt the whole financial system with wide-ranging implications from central banking to law and governance in the public sphere. The whitepaper is a vision document and preferred method for the founders of blockchain projects to describe the details of a project and its objectives.

The exponential rise in bitcoin price also helped those who entered early and gave them wealth and motivation to pursue loftier goals. During most of the last decade, it did not matter when you bought bitcoin, you would have made tremendous gains if you held on to it, as the bitcoin price has broken one record after another.

BITCOIN: THE SPARK OF CREATIVE DESTRUCTION

Bitcoin is a great victory for computer science, cryptography, and economics. Its foundations are built on ideas that have been in motion for over four decades. Several of the components that made Bitcoin possible—such as the use of cryptography to provide pseudonymous identities and digital signatures, blockchain as a tamper-evident data storage technique, and proof of work as a proxy for a vote in the virtual world to reach consensus—were developed in the last two to four decades. B-money, which was described in a paper published by Wei Dai in 1998, is quite close to Bitcoin in essence, even though it was never implemented and did not solve all the issues associated with decentralized digital cash.

It took a while for these concepts to form in the virtual world. Perhaps a major driver for the takeoff in Bitcoin technology was the advent of Web 2.0, where computing power is widely available, people around the world were interconnected through social media, and geographical boundaries melted. This made it easier for people with shared beliefs to come together. The early success of Bitcoin was primarily dominated by the crowd concerned about online privacy and freedoms.

The greatest innovation of Satoshi Nakamoto is not Bitcoin, though. Similarly, the greatest innovation of the Internet was not email, even though it was the first useful and important application. **The Bitcoin protocol, for the first time in**

human history, provides an autonomous manner to arrive at a consensus in a decentralized and trustless system.

Arriving at a consensus has been the basic fabric of modern society and achieved by giving people the power to vote, laying down the law, and building courts and governments to provide trust. In other words, centralization has been at the core of ensuring the social and legal contracts are respected and modern society functions as designed.

Modern institutions have had tremendous success in building nation-states and communities. Further, their impact can be seen in more wealth generation, higher life expectancy, and fewer wars than the world was experiencing only a hundred years ago.

One of the fundamental drivers of this success has been the technological innovation affecting all walks of life. It is also true the incumbent institutions miss out on disruptive innovations, as they focus on doing best on what is expected. Disruptive innovation starts at the fringes, bringing new entrants who serve a smaller segment often ignored by the incumbents. As the technology grows, the disruptor improves its performance on all the attributes and keeps its initial advantage, then the mainstream quickly moves to the disruptor, leaving behind the incumbent. As noted by Clayton Christensen, who was a professor at the Harvard Business School, this pattern has been quite common in the modern postindustrialization world.

Bitcoin protocol provides privacy and control to the individuals who care about them. That has not been the case with a significant majority of people, as can be seen by the billions who willingly give the details of their life to financial institutions and Internet companies such as

Visa, Mastercard, Facebook, and Instagram. For them, the ability to connect and share with others and the convenience of online transactions are far more important than the decentralization and trustless nature of Bitcoin protocol.

This will not always remain so. **The decentralization and trustless nature of the blockchain tremendously reduces the transaction cost element of an organization's many types of economic activity.** This is in addition to providing privacy and freedoms, which the proponents of Bitcoin protocol wanted. Therein lie the seeds of creative destruction that have the potential to unlock tremendous economic value, perhaps at a larger scale than the Internet itself.

As a new technology, Bitcoin has faced challenges in its path from the first transactions to the present moment when its market capitalization is more than double the largest bank in the United States, JPMorgan Chase.

However, explaining how Bitcoin and other cryptocurrencies looked different from the financial innovations of the past, Rich Rosenblum, president of crypto trading firm GSR, said, "Let's say credit derivatives was a new space that started in the early 2000s; you didn't have some of the most powerful people in tech having a Twitter handle, with like credit derivatives next to it. I think there's something special about crypto. It's a bit more of an asset and movement rather than just an asset class."

TEETHING ISSUES AND ARRIVAL OF NEW BLOCKCHAINS

Bitcoin's success brought its own difficulties. In 2015, the bitcoin block size, which was limited to one megabyte and created roughly every ten minutes, became insufficient for the large number of transactions taking place on the Bitcoin blockchain. This constraint meant many transactions would go unrecorded for a long time. Bitcoin protocol had no inbuilt mechanism to deal with such an issue. This scalability issue was followed by a big debate about the governance issues in decentralized autonomous organizations and how to resolve them.

Several solutions were proposed, including the simplest one, which was to increase the block size. However, given the protocol's decentralized nature and no inbuilt mechanism in the protocol itself to agree on the changes to the Bitcoin protocol and its code, the discussion mostly took place on message boards and chatrooms, and decisions were made on an ad hoc basis. The issue was finally resolved by increasing the block size, but the consensus was reached outside of the protocol itself. Once the fix was made to the core software, each participating node had to update its copy of the software. This brought forward a major issue with decentralized governance.

The governance debate also encouraged other programmers to propose new protocols which used the fundamental building blocks of the Bitcoin blockchain to solve more complex economic problems such as lending and borrowing.

WHAT NAKAMOTO CREATED

Leonard Kleinrock and his team provided the foundation of the Internet, which would one day support social media, e-commerce, banking, and much more. So, just like how Kleinrock's team at UCLA not only sent data from the computer at UCLA to another computer at the Stanford Research Institute, Satoshi invented more than bitcoin. Satoshi's work implied most of the organizational and economic activity could be disintermediated.

Satoshi's invention was by using proof of work. Consensus could be reached among a group of uncooperative computing nodes without the mediation of a third party. In the civic society, this third party is often a centralized authority such as the government, police, or court. In commerce, it is often the banks, lawyers, and courts.

Bitcoin supports a scripting language that allows the sender of bitcoins to encode instructions about how they should be spent. Such functionality allows one to create escrow accounts as well as insert conditions for the release and spending of bitcoins. The presence of this scripting language allows programmers to expand the capabilities of the Bitcoin protocols by building application layers on top of it.

THE PHILOSOPHER-KING ARRIVES

Bitcoin's success excited many programmers to create applications on top of the protocol, and many protocols such as Bitcoin Cash were born. Vitalik Buterin, a nineteen-year-old Russia-born Canadian programmer, realized Satoshi's ideas could be used for something much bigger. He conjectured that if he could create a blockchain that supported a Turing-complete scripting language, then applications of any complexity could be built on top of that blockchain. Named after Alan Turing, a programming language is said to be Turing-complete if it can handle instructions of any complexity.

Satoshi purposely kept the bitcoin scripting language Turing-incomplete to ensure the Bitcoin protocol supported one application, a peer-to-peer system of electronic transactions.

Buterin, fascinated by a possibility that could potentially upend how the Internet and financial industry worked, dropped out of the University of Waterloo and set out to write a whitepaper proposing such a version of Bitcoin on which applications of any complexity could be built. Such applications could provide more than just financial services. They could be used to create a decentralized version of Facebook, the stock market, and organizations of any complexity whose governance will be encoded on the blockchain.

In 2013, he presented a whitepaper proposing Ethereum. Ethereum went a step forward from Bitcoin, and instead of only being a ledger of coin transactions, it added another layer where the execution of computer code could be decentralized. The output of such execution will be the new state of the ledger.

The idea of executing contracts through computer programs came from Nick Szabo. In the true spirit of cypherpunks, Szabo envisioned a world in which legal contracts could be executed through computer code. Remember, cypherpunks wanted to create a society in which computer code, not the government-controlled money and enforced contracts. With smart contracts, Nick wanted to bring the practices of contract law to the world of e-commerce on the Internet, where these contracts could be entered into and executed without lawyers and courts. **Smart contracts are self-executing contracts that are written as computer code and executed by computers without the intervention of a trusted third party.**

THE ETHEREUM ICO

Buterin's whitepaper attracted widespread support from the community of developers. In January 2014, Buterin launched Ethereum at the North American Bitcoin Conference in Miami.

On July 22, 2014, an initial coin offering (ICO) was made. The Ethereum ICO raised fifty million dollars in forty-two days from the sale of ether (ETH), the cryptocurrency of the Ethereum platform, and would popularize this innovative fundraising model.

Ether is a native coin of the Ethereum platform, which is used to exchange value or make transactions on the platform. The interesting thing about ether cryptocurrency is it did not exist at the ICO's time. In an ICO, a project raises funds based on a whitepaper, which promises to issue the cryptocurrency to investors once the network is launched.

In 2015, the ERC-20 standard was released, which is a set of functions any smart contract or token created on Ethereum could implement. ERC stands for "Ethereum Request for Comment." Any application or blockchain network that handles the standard's functionality can integrate a token that implements the ERC-20 standard.

SMART CONTRACTS

In the Bitcoin network, the nodes are made of computerlike devices with the ability to perform computations. Ethereum takes the decentralized nature of the Bitcoin blockchain transactions one step further and allows for a more general case, in which the nodes execute a piece of code known as smart contracts in addition to sending cryptocurrency transactions.

A computer program takes some information such as data as an input and provides an output resulting from the computation the program was written to execute. So, the program is a static unit that can be distributed to the nodes in the network. These programs on the Ethereum network are known as smart contracts.

Let's take a closer look at "contract" to see how smart contracts can be valuable. The dictionary definition of the contract is as follows: "a written or spoken agreement... intended to be enforceable by law."

This means a contract is first agreed upon between the parties to the contract. There is a method that defines the execution of the contract. Finally, the successful execution of the contract requires a consensus among the parties to the contract.

The contract is enforceable by the law. This means if parties to the contract cannot reach a consensus, then the contract is interpreted in a court of law with attorneys' help. Once a judgment is passed, which resolves the contractual parties' conflicts, the resolution becomes enforceable by the law.

The legal system is the central entity in this process. This system has worked well and has been one of the pillars of modern democracy. However, there are significant costs to this system. These costs are primarily incurred in the creation, execution, consensus building, and enforcement of the contracts.

A smart contract is a set of instructions that encodes a contract's details, such as the conditions under which the contract is executed and what transactions take place at the contract execution. This code is based on carefully designed algorithms that encode all aspects of a contract, such as verification, negotiation, and enforcement.

The smart contract's unique aspect is its execution and enforcement is done by the computer code and not through the law.

The dictionary definition of a smart contract is: "code that facilitates, verifies, or enforces the negotiation or execution of a digital contract."

ETHEREUM: A DECENTRALIZED COMPUTER

According to the Ethereum website, "Ethereum is a decentralized platform designed to run smart contracts."

Like Bitcoin, Ethereum has a native asset called ether, which is the basis of value in the Ethereum ecosystem. This system uses it to align incentives among various participants.

Bitcoin and Ethereum are currently the most popular blockchain networks in the world. Their cryptocurrencies, bitcoin, and ether, are currently ranked number one and two by market cap.

Bitcoin blockchain was designed to support transactions in a decentralized manner. **The purpose of Ethereum is to be a smart contract execution platform, a decentralized distributed world computer.** Each node on the Ethereum network runs a software known as Ethereum Virtual Machine (EVM). This software can execute smart contracts.

A contract in the real world gets executed when certain conditions have been met. For example, an insurance contract known as weather derivatives pays a buyer a fixed amount of money at a fixed date if the temperature at a fixed location exceeds a fixed level. Once all these conditions are met, the seller of the contract transfers the agreed upon fixed amount in the contract to the buyer. If the conditions are not met, the contract expires and no exchange takes place.

This seemingly simple contract can be quite complex to execute, as many players get involved, ensuring the contract is correctly executed, and both parties are satisfied with the outcome. The complexity of executing this contract introduces a high cost the buyer of the contract must pay.

This contract could be executed on the Ethereum network in an autonomous manner, reducing the costs of verification, validation, enforcement, and money transfer as the computer code takes all these steps. There is no possibility of human, subjective judgment interfering with the original intent of the contract.

Ethereum network works similarly to the Bitcoin network except for the additional step of the EVM code execution. When a smart contract gets executed on the Ethereum network, all the participating nodes execute the code on their EVM and then compete to win the right to add the next block to the blockchain. In the same manner, like Bitcoin, a consensus is reached about the result of the smart contract's execution, and it is added to the blockchain. The result could be as simple as Alice paying Bob a certain amount of ether.

THE GAS FEE

The nodes participating in the Ethereum network get paid a fee in ether (ETH), also known as a gas fee. The nodes have a choice about which transactions to execute, and they try to maximize the fee they earn. This gives rise to imbalances on Ethereum for service demand on the network and the nodes executing transactions to facilitate these services. As the applications on top of the Ethereum network have proliferated, which use the Ethereum network to execute smart contracts, the gas prices have gone up significantly.

High gas prices on Ethereum imply there is huge demand from the application developers. Ethereum may be hitting boundary constraints in terms of its ability to facilitate transactions.

It is no surprise many other smart contract platforms are being developed to avoid the issues Ethereum is facing. Cardano—started by a cofounder of Ethereum, Charles Hoskinson—and Solana are two competitors.

In the next chapter, we will look at some of the popular applications of smart contracts, such as decentralized autonomous organizations (DAOs), decentralized finance (DeFi), and nonfungible tokens (NFTs).

CHAPTER 7

Decentralized Applications

———

"[Bitcoin] is a remarkable cryptographic achievement. The ability to create something which is not duplicable in the digital world has enormous value."

—ERIC SCHMIDT, FORMER CEO OF GOOGLE

The grand success of the Ethereum ICO and ERC-20 standard led to an ICO boom in 2017 when several projects raised billions of dollars in ICO using ERC-20 tokens. This increased the popularity of Ethereum and made it the de facto platform for developing decentralized applications, which will come to be known as dApps.

In some of the grandest fundraises through ICO, in May 2017, a web browser proposal for the decentralized web, called Brave, raised about thirty-five million dollars in less than thirty seconds. A messaging app developer company, Kik, raised about one hundred million dollars. In January 2018, while the crypto winter of a prolonged bear market was just beginning, Filecoin raised two hundred million dollars within the first hour of the cryptocurrency sale. According to *Forbes*, by October 2017, a total of about twenty billion dollars was raised by some eight hundred ICOs, 80 percent of which came from ERC-20 tokens on the Ethereum platform.

Block.one raised four billion dollars based only on a whitepaper to build a blockchain platform called EOS. A messaging app company, Telegram, raised 1.2 billion dollars. Both will later settle with the US securities regulators, and Telegram would agree to return the 1.2 billion dollars it raised from the investors.

Due to the unregulated nature of these offerings, many of the ICOs launched during the 2017 boom would turn out to be scams. According to *Fortune* magazine, about half of the ICOs launched during 2017 had failed by February 2018. The boom was finally stopped in its tracks by the regulatory authorities across the world going after scammers. The Securities and Exchange Commission (SEC) in the United States warned investors about the pump-and-dump in the ICO market. Pump-and-dump is a manipulation scheme in which insiders pump up the prices of a cryptocurrency by coordinating their buys, leading to a sharp price rise. Once the general public starts buying the cryptocurrency, often for fear of missing out (FOMO), the insiders dump their cryptocurrency, generating large profits for themselves. The dump causes a crash in the prices and leads to substantial losses for the other investors.

The then-SEC chairman, Jay Clayton, said during a hearing at US Congress, "I believe every ICO I've seen is a security," implying those involved in selling cryptocurrencies in ICOs may have offered securities illegally in the United States.

Many of the projects, though, will usher in a new era of cryptocurrencies. Satoshi's dream to disintermediate the financial system will carry on like a giant ship crashing through rocks and icebergs and pushing through to the new dawn of decentralized finance (DeFi).

In the previous chapters, we looked at various primitives that form the core of Bitcoin and Ethereum protocols. It is now time to consolidate that knowledge. In this chapter, we will look at various internal elements of a blockchain externally to develop a language about this technology which will deepen our understanding of how this all comes together. We will broaden our understanding of blockchain technology by learning about decentralized applications and some of their examples, such as decentralized autonomous organizations (DAOs) and decentralized finance (DeFi), which are natural extensions of the idea of a world computer.

Even though we have focused on Ethereum as the smart contract platform, many of the ideas developed with Ethereum will apply to other smart contract platforms such as Solana and Cardano. Each of these platforms tries to solve a "shortcoming" of Ethereum. So, if you understand Ethereum and its dApps ecosystem, you should understand any alternative to Ethereum existing, as well as those developed in the future. Ethereum continues to remain the top smart contract platform with the largest number of applications.

DECENTRALIZED APPLICATIONS (DAPPS)

Let's step back for a moment and think about what a computer is and how a distributed (world) computer expands on the power of a computer.

Most people think of a computer only as a PC or a laptop However, your smartphone is also a computing device. At its core, a computing device is made of hardware such as a microprocessor and software called an operating system (OS). An operating system (OS) provides a level of abstraction which allows software applications (apps) to interact with the hardware from a hand's distance. This allows application developers to write their applications for the OS, not the hardware. For example, if a video messaging application such as Skype is written for Windows OS, then it will run on any hardware (device) that has Windows OS installed. It could be your HP desktop or Dell laptop.

The job of OS is to provide a hardware-independent execution environment to computer programs written for that OS.

The Ethereum Virtual Machine (EVM) discussed in the previous chapter takes the concept of OS to another level of abstraction. The EVM sits between the smart contract, a program written in a programming language such as Solidity, and the OS. This ensures any Ethereum smart contract can run on any OS installed with the EVM.

The objective of the EVM is to allow any computing node to participate in Ethereum transactions, irrespective of what OS on whichever hardware they might have, making it possible for anyone with a computing device to participate in this network. By running the EVM on all the computing nodes in the network, Ethereum creates a distributed world computer where each computing node executes the same smart contract code in the same execution environment, the EVM. Once these nodes execute a smart contract code, they come to a consensus using the rules of the Ethereum protocols, making them look like they are part of the same computer.

This world computer can support any compatible application just like your Windows machine, MacBook, or iPhone support applications (apps) written for them.

Due to the decentralized nature of the execution environment of the apps built on top of the world computer, they are called decentralized applications, or dApps.

TOKENS

Cryptocurrencies are also known as tokens. Both names are used interchangeably. Bitcoin was the first cryptocurrency and application of blockchains. In the early part of the 2010s, many variations of Bitcoin protocol were created by forking the Bitcoin code and making improvements on that. You may have heard of Bitcoin Cash, Litecoin, etc. Other blockchains took the idea of the Bitcoin protocol and created blockchain protocols suited to specific use cases. For example, Tron was created to serve the media community, Brave was created as a decentralized web client, and Ethereum was created to become the world computer and support many applications. Most of the blockchains created in the public domain had a native token that would be used in the design of the incentive mechanism of the blockchain.

Equity tokens will provide pro rata ownership in the project.

Governance tokens will allow the token holders to participate in the governance votes for changes in the protocol allowed by its smart contracts.

Utility tokens will be needed to use the network.

Just like how your bank account is an updated record of all the transactions you have made with that account, a token account is a record of the token balances in each account.

Remember Ethereum has accounts, whereas Bitcoin only has transactions. But you get the idea—there is no physical equivalent to the tokens.

At the technical level, many types of tokens have been created. However, the category of fungible vs. nonfungible has become quite important due to its widespread applicability, as we will see later in this chapter.

FUNGIBLE TOKENS

A fungible token does not have any discriminating identity. This means one fungible token can be exchanged with another of the same value. An example of fungible tokens in the real world is the dollar bill—two five-dollar bills can be exchanged for a single ten-dollar bill.

In the Ethereum ecosystem, any token that implements the ERC-20 interface is fungible. This simple concept is very powerful. For example, DeFi protocol MakerDao has stablecoin DAI, which implements the ERC-20 interface. Once DAI implemented the ERC-20 interface, it could seamlessly integrate with other applications and protocols, even those not built yet. Currently, over 400 dApps have integrated with DAI. This interoperability allows the app developers to integrate with other applications and build services Lego-like seamlessly. The DeFi ecosystem is an example of this approach.

NONFUNGIBLE TOKENS (NFTS)

If a smart contract requires tokens with some unique characteristic, we will need tokens with a unique identity. For example, when digital art is created, the artist would want the art to have a unique identity which would make any copies of that digital art counterfeit. Nonfungible tokens can be used for this purpose, as they associate a unique identity to the art piece.

Nonfungible tokens have become very important in gaming and the art world. They are also very useful in DeFi when unique security is needed, like if a borrower in DeFi has a customized interest rate and payment schedule.

Nonfungible tokens implement the ERC-721 interface of the Ethereum protocol.

DECENTRALIZED FINANCE (DEFI)

Satoshi wanted to disintermediate banks from the payment systems and central banks from the mint. The foundational nature of Satoshi's ideas can be seen in the use cases that were not imagined by the cypherpunks.

Decentralized finance is an application built on top of the Ethereum network, which does not rely on central intermediaries such as banks, brokerages, and exchanges to offer traditional financial products, instead utilizing smart contracts. The DeFi platform allows people to buy and sell insurance and derivative contracts, lend and borrow, and speculate on price movements on a variety of assets. This application started in 2020, and by mid-November 2021, more than 250 billion dollars were locked on the DeFi platform.

There are currently many protocols such as MakerDAO, Compound, Curve, dYdX, Uniswap, etc., which form the crowded DeFi ecosystem. We will look at one of the earliest and more ubiquitous platforms—the MakerDAO. Once you understand the core ideas behind MakerDAO, you should be able to broaden your knowledge of other DeFi protocols such as Compound, AAVE, and Uniswap, as the core ideas behind most of them remain the same.

MAKERDAO

The Maker protocol was started as an open-source project in 2014 with the objective of providing a permission-less borrowing and lending platform and loans backed by cryptocurrencies.

In 2015, Rune Christensen, a Danish entrepreneur, created MakerDAO. Unlike many cryptocurrency projects which took advantage of the 2017 ICO boom, MakerDAO chose the VC route instead. It raised more than fifty million dollars throughout the platform development and has been backed by the likes of Andreessen Horowitz.

MakerDAO has followed a typical path followed by many of the successful DeFi protocols such as Compound, Curve, dYdX, and Uniswap. Its protocol, built on the Ethereum smart contract platform, consists of a governance token, MKR (known as "maker"), and a stablecoin, DAI (named after Wei Dai of b-money fame).

MakerDAO began similar to a privately owned tech startup and then transitioned to decentralized governance. In the beginning, a limited number of tokens were distributed among the founders, development team, and investors. For example, Andreessen Horowitz took 6 percent of all MKR tokens available for an investment of fifteen million dollars.

MakerDAO used the funds raised from the VCs to develop the protocol. The project was managed by the MakerDAO Foundation, which took control of the project. Once the development work was complete and the network was operating as expected, MakerDAO Foundation was dissolved, and the holders of MKR tokens managed the network in a fully decentralized manner according to a smart contract-based decentralized autonomous organization (DAO).

Unlike an investment in a start-up, MKR tokens can be freely traded on cryptocurrency exchanges such as Coinbase and Binance.

THE DESIGN OF MAKERDAO

MakerDAO protocol consists of two tokens: a governance token, MKR, discussed above, and a stablecoin, DAI. A **stablecoin** is a token whose price is pegged against the value of a stable asset, such as the US dollar, gold, or other commodities. The value of DAI is soft pegged against the US dollar while an algorithm maintains the peg. In a soft peg, a currency's exchange rate is maintained by economic incentives that drive supply and demand in the market to keep the currency's value pegged to the stable asset. DAI can be purchased from centralized exchanges such as Coinbase and Binance or decentralized exchanges (DEX) such as Uniswap and Curve. DAI is minted on MakerDAO.

DAI is an ERC-20 token. You can deposit an ERC-20 token in a smart contract known as Maker Collateral Vaults and mint DAI depending on the collateralization ratio of the deposit asset. For example, the collateralization ratio for ETH is 150 percent, which means for every one-thousand-dollar ETH deposit, you can borrow (or mint) 666.7 DAI (=1,000 dollars/1.5). You can sell these DAI on a centralized or decentralized exchange, use it to buy a cryptocurrency, or convert it to US dollars on Coinbase, transfer to your bank account, and use it as a down payment for your home loan. You can alternatively deposit your DAI on another lending platform, such as Compound, and earn interest on it. Once you return your borrowed DAI to the vault, the smart contract releases your collateral back to you.

You need to ensure the value of your collateral remains higher than that demanded by the collateralization ratio. Otherwise, some or all of your collateral will get liquidated by the smart contracts to bring your collateralization ratio back in line.

This simple example shows how you can generate additional yield on your cryptocurrencies. The parameters, such as which tokens to add to the list of collateral on MakerDAO or collateralization ratio of individual assets, are approved by the decentralized MakerDAO governance. Anyone can propose a change to the protocol allowed by the smart contract of the protocol. The MKR holders can then vote on the proposal.

Several ERC-20 tokens, such as ETH, are currently supported as collateral, and more are added regularly. MakerDAO was one of the earliest DeFi applications to launch on Ethereum. Its stablecoin, DAI, was an innovation, as its peg to the US dollar is managed by computer code in a fully transparent manner and independent of a central entity.

There are many stablecoins, such as tether (USDT), the fourth largest cryptocurrency at the time of writing. USDT has a fixed peg to the US dollar, and it is issued by a Hong Kong-based company, Tether. As per Tether, USDT's peg is maintained by holding equal assets in dollar terms such as commercial paper, reverse repo notes, treasury bills, and cash. You have to trust Tether, though, to maintain that peg. Unfortunately, Tether has not agreed to do a full audit of its account. It has been previously sued by the New York attorney general's office, which Tether settled without admitting any wrongdoing.

DAI and Maker are also composable, which means other developers can see their code, write applications for them, and extend their functionality. This composability has led to a proliferation of applications built around the MakerDAO ecosystem. For example, DAI allows the development of decentralized exchanges, which enables assets to trade against DAI, a stablecoin, instead of another cryptocurrency such as bitcoin, reducing volatility in the price of the traded pairs.

There is no central person or entity anywhere on the MakerDAO network. It will have more than ten billion dollars locked on the platform in early October 2021, and more than four hundred platforms have integrated the DAI token.

The DeFi platforms have exploded in the past two years, as the total value locked on these platforms has ballooned to over 250 billion dollars. The decentralization in finance has arrived.

THE DISRUPTION ECONOMY

In the blockchain economy, disruption is a common theme. Bitcoin started as the first blockchain network, but soon, Ethereum was developed to support more complex transactions, followed by others such as Cardano and Solana. The rapid pace of applications built on top of these protocols, such as the Compound DeFi application on top of Ethereum, further complicates the predictability of the ultimate winners. This was like the early phases of the Internet growth when there were several competitors in search, social media, and e-commerce. Who will be the last ones standing will be determined by how they respond to challenges posed by competitors. In the next section, we will delve deeper into economic theories that shed light on these issues.

PART 3

THE VENTURE CAPITAL ANALYST

Projects behind cryptocurrencies are tech start-ups. This section will look at a few qualitative tools that help develop scenarios about how a crypto project will evolve in the future.

By the end of this section, you will learn:

- How the high-tech world shows increasing marginal returns, i.e., what is big gets bigger.

- How the network properties determine which blockchain protocol will capture market share.

- How to apply the theory of disruption to understand the evolution and structure of the crypto economy.

CHAPTER 8

A Tale of Two Economies

———

"The central event of the twentieth century is the overthrow of matter."

—GEORGE GILDER

It took Apple forty-two years to reach a market cap of one trillion dollars. Bitcoin achieved that feat in twelve years. The largest bank in the US, JPMorgan Chase & Co., whose history stretches back to 1799, reached its historical market cap peak of about 517 billion dollars in October 2021.

What causes some products, platforms, and companies to grow exponentially while most follow a more somber combination of S-curve? In an S-curve growth, a product grows slowly in the beginning, followed by an accelerating pace of adoption before flattening out as the market demand is saturated. To achieve further growth, the product has to find new markets or make significant improvements, both of which cost money and time.

If you look at cryptocurrencies in terms of price and the number of participants in the network, the growth has been phenomenal. By all means, the cryptocurrencies and their underlying platforms are not the only technology to have seen exponential growth. Others, like Facebook, have followed a similar trajectory. However, the speed with which so many crypto projects have grown together is unprecedented. Take DeFi, for example—the first decentralized stablecoin DAI was launched on Ethereum in December 2017. By October 2021, the total value locked (TVL) on various DeFi protocols is more than two hundred billion dollars. You can think of TVL as the asset under management (AUM) on these platforms.

To understand the value drivers behind cryptocurrencies, you need to have familiarity with the basic rules of economics that govern the growth of these protocols. Most of the people are trained in a branch of economics unsuitable for networks. In fact, application of the tools of classical economics to high technology companies, especially those with network effects such as Uber and Facebook, has led to undervaluation by a majority of investors during the early high-growth phases of these companies, denying them high returns experienced by the stocks of these companies. The experience of these investors with cryptocurrencies is even worse.

A FORK IN THE ROAD

At the turn of the millennium, the composition of the western economies had a significant split. On the one hand, they were the economy companies of age-old industries that spawned in the early part of the previous century as industrialization took place across the western world. On the other hand, the new economy industries were powered by the sharing and processing of information using the advances in information technologies.

The second industrial revolution that had started in the late nineteenth century gave way to widespread adoption of technologies such as telegraph, railroad networks, and electrical power, driven by advancements in manufacturing and production technologies. The telephone and road networks further increased the mobility of people and ideas. The advancements in agriculture driven by better tools and machinery brought food security to the masses.

In the latter half of the twentieth century, the world economy shifted from mechanical and analog to the digital economy, characterized by the widespread adoption of computers and digital recordkeeping. This era was defined by the coexistence of the old world of manufacturing and the new world of information processing that brought a shift in a significant part of the economy from bulk processing to design and use of technology.

The growth during the second industrial revolution led to a better understanding of the economics of production. The leading English economist, Alfred Marshall, wrote his seminal book, *Principles of Economics*, in 1890. This remained a dominant textbook in England and continental Europe for many decades and built the key ideas of supply and demand, cost of production, the theory of diminishing returns, and market equilibrium. Marshall's work had a significant influence on economists who followed him.

Economics and the framework of learning and evaluating the components of economies such as the firms, products, and technologies continued to rely on Marshall's ideas and its intellectual successors. The same tools have been applied to study the firms and products in the information processing world.

THE OLD ECONOMY AND DIMINISHING MARGINAL RETURNS

W. Brian Arthur, an economist who developed the modern approach to increasing returns, wrote an influential article in *Harvard Business Review* titled "Increasing Returns and the New World of Business," in which Brian contrasts the old economy of diminishing returns and the new economy of increasing returns. Many of his ideas are relevant to the nature of blockchain networks, which show increasing marginal returns.

One of Marshall's major ideas was the theory of diminishing returns that was the foundation of most of his work on the theory of the firm and cost of production. For more than a century, Marshall's thinking has informed our understanding of how firms and markets work.

According to the theory, there is an optimal capacity beyond which incremental inputs to a production process will result in diminishing returns—**we get less extra output when we add additional units of an input holding other inputs fixed.** For example, as more workers are added to a factory floor, the additional worker has less space, materials, and machinery to work with, if these inputs are fixed. The factory floor gets crowded, the machinery is overworked, and the marginal output of the worker declines.

Marshall inhabited a world of bulk production consisting of agriculture, ore processing, metal making, and chemical manufacturing, which relied heavily on repeatable production processes and were light on information processing. There was a limit to growth dictated by the scarcity of one or more input resources in this world. For example, if you put too many seeds in the ground, eventually, each additional increment of seeds yields less than the previous one, as the land becomes crowded.

Marshall's ideas continue to live mostly within the bulk processing part of the modern economy. A few players who continue to optimize the production process now dominate the markets as opposed to Marshall's world of perfect competition. Product differentiation and brand names have led to a smaller set of companies in most of these markets. These companies still face limitations on access to raw materials, consumers, or availability of one or more inputs, leading to thin profit margins and limited profit opportunities. These limitations on inputs and profit margins mean no one company can make a killing.

The old economy part of the modern-day markets continues to behave in a stable and predictive manner, making them amenable to scientific analysis. The predictability allows economists and financial analysts to use history of production and consumption patterns to predict the future costs, revenue, and profitability of the companies operating in these markets, making a financial valuation tool like discounted cash flow (DCF) analysis applicable.

THE NEW ECONOMY AND INCREASING MARGINAL RETURNS

In contrast to the old economy, many products and companies in the knowledge economy have different dynamics of growth due to network effects that lead to increasing marginal returns.

There is a high ceiling on how much a company or product can grow in the world of increasing marginal returns. The product in the new economy is often a technology based on information. Once created, it can be shared or distributed at a very low-cost. The network effects show when the product becomes more valuable as more people use it. Contrast this to the old economy, where a product available to everyone is less valuable than the one with limited availability. Rolls-Royce, a high-end car in the luxury segment owned by BMW, sells about four thousand units every year and charges more than three hundred thousand per car. In contrast, BMW makes about a quarter-million vehicle sales per year, with prices ranging from thirty to one hundred thousand dollars. In addition to quality, scarcity leads to value in this part of the economy. Each new unit becomes less valuable, showing decreasing marginal returns.

In the digital world, operating systems (OSs) show increasing marginal returns. The OS manages hardware and software resources of computing devices, such as personal computers and smartphones, and provides common services for the user applications running on these devices, such as a spreadsheet software or messaging app. The power of the OS comes from separating the user application from the underlying hardware. An application written for a Windows OS will run on any machine that has Windows OS installed irrespective of whether the hardware is an IBM PC or Dell laptop.

THE OPERATING SYSTEM WARS

In the early 1980s, the operating system (OS) market for personal computers was heating up. The arrival of the IBM PC in 1981 put computers in people's homes. According to a story of mythical proportions in Silicon Valley, at the beginning of the 1980s, IBM reached out to Bill Gates and asked him to build an OS for its new personal computer (PC) project.

At the time, computers were primarily used by industries and academia. Gates was running a Seattle based start-up, Microsoft, which he had cofounded in 1975 with Paul Allen. Microsoft was a small start-up and primarily wrote programming language interpreters. Gates did not have an OS, so he asked IBM to approach Gary Kildall to discuss a potential licensing agreement for the use of the CP/M operating system with IBM PC.

In the '70s, the leading operating system was CP/M, also known as Control Program for Microcomputers, developed by Digital Research, Inc. It was written by a tech pioneer, Gary Kildall, who did the early work on operating systems. CP/M was the first mass-market operating system introduced in 1974. By 1979, it had become the dominant OS and was widely used in businesses through the late 1970s and early 1980s.

The legend goes that the IBM executives could not get a meeting with Gary Kildall, as he was flying his plane, and were asked to meet Mrs. Kildall instead. The meeting fell off, though, as Mrs. Kildall declined to sign a nondisclosure agreement that looked too broad to her. An alternative thread of the story is IBM did talk to Gary, but the deal fell off as Gary wanted more than a two-hundred-thousand-dollar flat license fee in perpetuity, which IBM was offering for his OS. Then IBM gave a contract to Microsoft to build an operating system from scratch. This would turn out to be a seismic event that would put Microsoft near the center of the global information age for decades to come (Greene, 2014).

At the time of receiving the IBM contract, Microsoft had never developed an operating system, so it looked around and bought QDOS, the "Quick and Dirty Operating System," for fifty thousand dollars from Tim Paterson, a Seattle based computer programmer.

In an ironic twist of fate, Tim Paterson used the CP/M manual to write his operating system in about six weeks. Microsoft built PC-DOS for IBM based on QDOS. Gates talked IBM into letting Microsoft keep the distribution rights of DOS and named MS-DOS "the Microsoft Disk Operating System, its OS for non-IBM PCs."

By 1984, Apple's Mac had arrived. IBM PC's DOS was a kludge and known to be buggy. The Mac OS was far easier to use and more stable than any other OS. But the battle of operating systems was still undecided (*Forbes*, 1997).

THE NETWORK EFFECT

Microsoft's deal with IBM gave its hastily assembled and known to be buggy OS a large platform to spread. Microsoft also allowed outside developers to write user applications for MS-DOS. With IBM PC's success, Microsoft was able to attract developers to build user application software for MS-DOS, as developers saw the benefit of writing for MS-DOS—an OS for a popular computer. Software success often depends on whether it can attract a network of software developers and users.

For example, the growing base of IBM PC users led Lotus Software to write spreadsheet software for MS-DOS, which grew in value as more users shared information in a spreadsheet format. You can see the network effect play both at the level of MS-DOS and the spreadsheet software. Both become more valuable with every new user. A new user could potentially share information in spreadsheet format with all the existing users, so there's marginally more value in spreadsheets and MS-DOS to the new user than to the previously added user. This marginal improvement in the value of the product is driven by network effects which create increasing returns with the addition of new developers who write software for MS-DOS and each new user of the application developed by these developers.

The increasing base of developers and users also forced hardware providers to adapt to MS-DOS, and by 1990, it had become the dominant OS in the PC market. The network effects helped MS-DOS replace CP/M as the leading provider of operating systems. Microsoft also had a significant head start on Mac due to these network effects.

Even though Mac OS was superior in stability and design, MS-DOS was able to get ahead by keeping its system open to outside developers and locking in the majority of the market. This open system attracted outside developers to write software for its OS. On the other hand, Mac remained a closed system and did not allow outside developers to write software for its OS, losing out on the value created by the network of developers.

The main drivers of network effects are as follows (Arthur, 1996):

POSITIVE FEEDBACK LOOPS

Due to their inherent positive feedback loops, networks can have an exponential growth in the userbase. In a positive feedback system, an increase in input causes output growth, which in turn leads to an increase in the input, and the loop continues. MS-DOS attracted more developers of user applications, increasing the number of applications on its platform. An increase in the userbase of MS-DOS attracted more developers to write software for MS-DOS.

PRODUCT ECOLOGY

Technology products often exist within a mini-ecology of several products. These ecologies can be thought of as a web of loose alliances that enhance each other through positive feedback in the network, benefiting the base. During the OS wars, Apple came up with a superior OS compared to the other offerings, but it closed off its OS and did not build an ecology around it. Microsoft came out spectacularly successful due to the mini-ecology it created around MS-DOS. Microsoft ecology was built around personal computing for individual users as opposed to the industrial computing that was the primary use of computers in the '70s. By aligning itself closely with the most popular personal computer—IBM PC—and software developers like Lotus Software, Microsoft successfully created a mini-ecology crucial in fending off competitors such as Mac OS and CP/M. It completely replaced CP/M by the mid-'80s and became a dominant player in the OS market by capturing over 90 percent of the market. Apple's Mac OS continued to have a much smaller share of the OS market, as it did not create alliances and alignments with other software and hardware providers, choosing to go alone instead.

SWITCHING COSTS

By building a large community of developers writing software for MS-DOS, Microsoft was able to lock in the users. The users switching from MS-DOS would not find many of the applications they had become used to with MS-DOS. Since Apple was building its own suite of applications for Mac OS, it would not be able to keep up with Microsoft, which relied on both in-house and outside developers for user application software.

MAKING SENSE OF IT ALL

In Marshall's smokestack economy of bulk processing, no company or product could corner the market as marginal returns went down with the number of units produced. In the new information processing economy, the opposite is true. Each new user of a new economy product would create more value for the next, as the network effects create positive feedback, making it more valuable for the suppliers and developers of the peripheral products. In the case of MS-DOS, these would be the hardware manufacturers and software developers. Further, the company would be able to divide upfront costs among a larger number of users.

"Increasing returns are the tendency for that which is ahead to get further ahead, for that which loses advantage to lose further advantage. They are mechanisms of positive feedback that operate—within markets, businesses, and industries—to reinforce that which gains success or aggravates that which suffers a loss. Increasing returns generate not equilibrium but instability. If a product, company, or technology—one of many competing in a market—gets ahead by chance or clever strategy, increasing returns can magnify this advantage, and the product, company, or technology can go on to lock in the market" (Arthur, 1994).

The world of increasing returns is quite unpredictable, with a lot of unknowns. In the case of the operating system wars, it was MS-DOS that dethroned the only dominant player, CP/M, in a very short period, as it built alliances and a product ecology. In such a world, product superiority alone does not ensure dominance. MS-DOS was inferior to Apple's Mac OS, but Mac had only 8 percent of the OS market while MS-DOS had 90 percent.

Microsoft's dominance in the OS market helped its investors make a killing and turned Gates into the richest person on earth for more than two decades. When Microsoft went public in an IPO in 1986, it created three billionaires and twelve thousand millionaires.

In 1980, it would not have been possible to predict the astronomical growth Microsoft would achieve through its fifty-thousand-dollar purchase of QDOS—Quick and Dirty Operating System. This would have made it very hard to make any reasonable financial projections for the firm that would provide a reasonable value of Microsoft to an investor.

THE CASINO OF TECHNOLOGY

How do investors position themselves in an increasing marginal return economy? "The ability to profit under increasing returns is only as good as the ability to see what's coming in the next cycle and to position oneself for it—technologically, psychologically, and cooperatively," said W. Brian Arthur.

A technology manager or investor in such an economy is like a player in the knowledge industry casino. In the bulk processing world of the old economy, what mattered to the investors was how a company capitalized on its core competencies, reduced cost, improved quality, and whether it priced its products competitively. In today's knowledge-based world, the primary driver of growth is the special economics of positive feedback. The investor in this economy is not playing a game of poker. Instead, **the game is in a casino where the investor needs to decide how much to stake on which table, when to double down, and when to fold.**

CHAPTER 9

Network, Network, Network

"The First Law: Performance drives success, but when performance can't be measured, networks drive success."

—ALBERT-LÁSZLÓ BARABÁSI, *THE FORMULA:*

THE UNIVERSAL LAWS OF SUCCESS

The new economy companies Uber, Facebook, and Airbnb all benefited from network effects and have shown steep growth over their first decade of existence. Where Facebook has come to dominate social networking and Airbnb in rentals, Uber has faced strong competition. Uber investors such as Bill Gurley of Benchmark, a venture capital firm, believed Uber would take all of the market share in the car-for-hire market due to its first mover advantage and network effects. As we will see in a later chapter, Bill valued Uber at 150 billion dollars, but Uber has not realized that level of valuation and has faced stiff competition in various markets across the world.

What made Facebook capture the global social media market while Uber failed to do so? This insight is central to the network analysis of blockchain networks because it allows us to decide which networks will be like Facebook and Airbnb, which will be like Uber, and of course, which will be Myspace, a social media company before Facebook. This will have an important impact on the value we assign to each network. This value will form the basis of investments in these projects.

Not all networks are the same. Networks have properties that differentiate them from each other. In a *Harvard Business Review* article titled "Why Some Platforms Thrive and Others Don't," the author duo Feng Zhu and Marco Iansiti identified five fundamental properties of networks. These properties are the strength of networks, clustering in the network, bridging of multiple networks, risk of disintermediation, and vulnerability to multihoming.

STRENGTH OF NETWORKS

Facebook and Uber both rely on network effects to create and capture economic value. However, the two networks have different strengths. If your friends are on Facebook, the value of being on Facebook is higher for you compared to when nobody you knew was on Facebook. Uber, on the other hand, has local network effects. When more people join Uber's network in a city, the drivers benefit due to lower wait times, and this prompts more drivers to join Uber's network, enhancing liquidity and prompting more users to join Uber. Unless people from other cities travel to this city, this growth of users and drivers on Uber's platform in one city does not generally increase value for the people in other cities, leading to only strong local network effects for Uber.

Due to its weak global network effects, Uber has different competitors in different locations. In the United States, Uber is competing with Lyft in addition to smaller local players in cities. In China, Uber was kicked out of the country by Didi. In India, it continues to compete with the global rival, Lyft, and local giant, Ola. Facebook, on the other hand, has almost a monopoly across the world, supported by its popular products such as Instagram and WhatsApp.

Network effects rise and fall with time as the market structure and technology ecosystem change. In the '80s and early '90s, Microsoft's operating system, MS-DOS, was ubiquitous. Its lead was supported by the app developers who wrote for the MS-DOS and later for its Windows operating system. Microsoft had locked in the OS market because the apps resided on its OS. By the late '90s and early 2000s, developers started writing apps that supported cross-operating systems and resided on the Internet. This gave a quick rise to multiple OS networks such as Windows, Android, iOS, and Mac OS.

CLUSTERING IN THE NETWORK

Uber's localized networks create local clusters. Clustering means a competitor to Uber can try to gain a critical mass at the local level and compete with Uber without needing to enter the market on a global scale. This is how Ola in India and Didi in China had gained significant market share even though Uber had a global scale when these players entered their local markets. On a more localized scale, Uber is facing competition from taxi companies in New York and San Francisco as they move their business online.

Facebook, on the other hand, has a global appeal. The global diversity of people on the Facebook platform makes it more interesting from a content perspective. In a globalized economy, people of different nationalities are sprinkled around the world. Facebook and its products, such as Instagram, continue to give this diaspora home experience from a content perspective. Any competitor to Facebook will need to enter the social media market at a global scale to capture the global nature of its network, a task much harder than taking on Uber in a city such as New York.

BRIDGING OF MULTIPLE NETWORKS

A successful platform can attract a large number of customers and then collect an enormous amount of data on the activity of these customers. By studying customers' interactions with the platform, service providers, and other users, a platform can create an in-depth profile of its users and their preferences. This profiling allows the platform to expand into different verticals.

Amazon started by selling books online. It tracked the users' actions on its platform to create a recommender system showing the books to customers the system thought they were more likely to buy. As the customer more readily found the books they liked, they would leave reviews on the website, which were helpful to other potential book buyers.

This demand-side network on Amazon and the profile data of the buyers gave rise to a supply-side network and attracted sellers of many other goods. The sellers could further identify the popular products on Amazon and efficiently manage their inventory. Amazon used its success in building a strong network of buyers and sellers to create prime services that provide free shipping to frequent buyers who would, in turn, buy more due to the reduced cost of purchasing goods on Amazon's platform. Amazon further expanded its prime services to videos, shows, and movies.

Chinese online giant Alibaba has similarly expanded in e-commerce, financing, and payments businesses, using success in one vertical and the acquired network to provide services in other verticals, leveraging its network to multiply its businesses.

RISK OF DISINTERMEDIATION

Homejoy, a cleaning company, started as an online platform connecting cleaners and homeowners who required cleaning services. Flush with cash from a recent thirty-eight-million-dollar raise, Homejoy wanted to build a network that would create a critical mass necessary for a winner-takes-it-all success, like other aggressive start-ups. The company started by offering a steep discount to its early customers. It cut the price to nineteen dollars for 2.5 hours of cleaning, originally worth eighty-five dollars.

Homejoy did not realize, though, the network it was building had poor properties. Once the initial discount period was over, the users quickly disappeared, often directly contracting with the cleaners. On the other hand, the cleaners had no use of Homejoy's services once they had a full roster of clients.

Homejoy's network had a fatal flaw—the potential of disintermediation. Once the buyers and sellers of cleaning services met, they had no incentive to continue interacting through Homejoy after the discount period was over. This was reflected in Homejoy's customer retention of 15 to 20 percent. By 2015, Homejoy burned through most of its cash pile; a Silicon Valley darling just a few years back, it had to shutter its doors for good (Zhu et al. 2019).

VULNERABILITY TO MULTIHOMING

When the cost of onboarding multiple platforms is low for the platforms' users, they end up signing with multiple platforms. Many customers use both Uber and Lyft to compare prices and reduce wait times. This property of market networks, known as multihoming, makes it difficult for a successful platform to continue to grow boundlessly. Competitors may try to lock in smaller clusters in a network by focusing their resources on those clusters. Uber and Lyft often focus their promotions on smaller geographies, indicating they want to reduce multihoming by establishing themselves into individual clusters.

NETWORK PROPERTIES ARE A KEY

Suppose you want to understand how a blockchain network such as Bitcoin, Ethereum, or Solana will win in a market and whether that victory will be fleeting or lasting. In that case, you need to identify the network in which a protocol is embedded. You will need to look at the properties of this network to see whether the network is weak or strong, has localized clusters that competitors can attack, and whether it can bridge multiple networks. And if there is a risk of network users interacting directly and leaving the network after the initial handshake.

A company's product offering can often be designed using the network properties in mind. It is important to understand a product may help create the network, but it cannot control it forever. As social media companies Friendster, Myspace, and Orkut have shown, the networks will continue to exist beyond the life of a product. They can be leveraged to create bigger networks as Amazon did, but they can also be taken over by a new product such as Facebook.

The idea of increasing marginal returns has its limitations. Once a product has helped establish a network, the ecosystem of products around the network can also continue to grow, often at an exponential rate. Some of these products can spawn their own ecosystem, which can take away the advantage of the incumbent leader in the network and give rise to more nimble and innovative players who can kick out the incumbent and become the disruptive leader.

During the '90s, Microsoft had a monopoly over the OS market due to the network of six million apps created by the software developers who wanted their apps to reside on the most popular OS. Microsoft's OS dominance quickly vanished once Web 2.0 took off during the first decade of this millennium. The cloud made it possible for the data and applications to reside and be delivered on the Internet. Microsoft's once-formidable monopoly was challenged by competing OS platforms, many of which have become coleaders in their segments, such as Android and iOS on smartphones and Mac and Windows on laptops and PC. This shows network strength can vary with time.

SWITCHING COSTS AND NETWORK DEFENSIBILITY

Networks once established introduce switching costs for their users. For example, if someone created a new social media platform like Facebook, you would not want to join it because nobody from your network was there yet. Unless all your friends and their friends moved to the new platform, the switching cost would be too high.

Switching cost is an important consideration in many technology products. When you learn the ropes and tricks of an operating system like Microsoft Windows, it will become difficult for you to switch to Mac, even if it has a better user interface.

Once a product eschews a network, it creates a switching cost for its users, as the size of the network is often a determinant to the network's value. Per Metcalfe's law, the value of a network is proportional to the square of the network size. As a network becomes large, it creates value for all its participants. If a participant leaves, she loses the value provided by the network. The network value to this participant becomes a switching cost for her.

The switching cost creates network defensibility. The higher the switching cost, the more defensible the network is. The switching costs also allow the network provider to charge a fee from the participants. The users will pay the fee as long as it is lower than the switching cost (Walden, 2020).

THE ECONOMICS OF CRYPTO NETWORKS

One common criticism of bitcoin and other cryptocurrencies is their protocols are based on open-source code. The source code is openly available to everyone, not by accident but by design. The public blockchain networks are decentralized, achieved in part by allowing anyone to download the protocol. The governance in these protocols is achieved by a consensus mechanism, which also necessitates the underlying code to be transparent to the participants.

When you create value in a network based on open-source code, there is always a possibility the code can be copied, and a competing network can be created. In the case of protocols such as Bitcoin and Ethereum, this is not only possible but has already happened many times.

The open-source code is more like a blueprint on which a network is built. The code behind blockchain platforms is dead until users start joining the network and interacting with the platform and each other. These interactions add data to the code, bringing it to life. Data is what gives the code life. The quantity and quality of data on the networks depend on the quality and quantity of the stakeholders on the networks and their interactions. If Elon Musk and Michael Saylor buy into bitcoin, then the quality of the network rises far more than when I joined the bitcoin network by purchasing my first one hundred dollars of satoshis.

Similarly, when Tesla invested more than one billion dollars from its treasury in bitcoin, that single entity brought a lot more value to the network than a new retail buyer of bitcoin.

HOW CRYPTOCURRENCIES IMPACT THE NETWORK PROPERTIES

Cryptocurrencies expand on the idea of traditional economic networks such as Facebook. Facebook makes hundreds of billions of dollars every year by monetizing the chatter of its participants. These Facebook participants writing, commenting, liking, clapping, and swiping on their smartphones do not make a dime.

Suppose a new social media company started by offering its network participants a cut in the pie they helped create. What do you think would happen? The barrier created by switching costs would become surmountable by the value to the participants gained from sharing in the revenue of the new social media platform.

The implication of cryptocurrencies is they allow their network participants to share the value of the network. This incentivizes participants to contribute as much as they can to enhance the network value. Furthermore, the miners will provide more computing power to safeguard the network. The investors will make positive comments to influence more people to join the network. The software developers will enhance and maintain the protocol code to provide expected services in the best manner. Any security vulnerability is resolved before malicious actors can exploit it.

THE BITCOIN NETWORK

The Bitcoin network began as a decentralized alternative payments system. The high volatility of bitcoin and the slower speed of transaction settlement as each new block was added roughly every ten minutes made bitcoin unappealing as a payment currency. There are various efforts underway to enhance the speed of transaction settlements. Also, the messaging protocol SWIFT, created in the 1970s, does not do final settlements instantly. Visa and Mastercard often tout their payment networks' speed of transaction as superior to Bitcoin. This is not completely true, as any merchant would tell you. Normally a merchant receives payments made by credit cards in a day or more. If you ever returned merchandise at a store, you may remember it was several days before the refund was returned to your account.

The Lightning protocol of Bitcoin is a solution where trusted counterparties can make the settlement off-blockchain, then the transaction will be settled on the blockchain with some delay—usually a few minutes. Meanwhile, the price volatility problem of bitcoin will be solved as the cryptocurrency becomes widely adopted.

Until bitcoin becomes a preferred technology backbone for payments, it will continue to serve as another important function—a store of value. Mike Novogratz said, "I feel really strongly bitcoin's best usage is as a store of value. Its best chance of success is staying in that lane and not trying to be everything else." He added, "So if you're a maximalist, you're like, 'Oh, we're gonna have payments on the Lightning Network, and this new upgrade called taproot and schorr is going to make it more programmable.' All that stuff is bad for bitcoin because we've convinced the world it works perfectly the way it is as digital gold.

"It doesn't need low transaction cost to be digital gold. It just needs to be bitcoin, like it is today. If you want it to be everything, you're going to have to fundamentally change it. The moment you say you want to be a currency for payments, every regulator in the world's going to tell you to stand down," said Mike.

Many of the early proponents of bitcoin, such as Tim Draper, Anthony "Pomp" Pompliano, and Mike Novogratz, saw bitcoin as an alternative store of value. Recently, many large and famous hedge fund investors like Stanley Druckenmiller and Paul Tudor Jones have invested 2 to 4 percent of their wealth in bitcoin, which can be hundreds of millions. The addition of these high-value participants to the Bitcoin network has led to more acceptance of bitcoin among the institutional investors, many of which are now planning to add bitcoin to their portfolios.

THE COMPETITION TO BITCOIN

Bitcoin's current success is due to being seen as a store of value by most long-term holders. It may become a medium of exchange in the long-term, but that is not a prerequisite for its ultimate success. The Bitcoin clones, on the other hand, are primarily competing as a peer-to-peer payment alternative with minor improvements that aim to solve some deficiencies of the Bitcoin protocol. Many solutions have been proposed to speed up settlement times on the Bitcoin network.

The institutional infrastructure, such as custody, audit, and derivative products that have been built around bitcoin, is much larger than any other cryptocurrency, which makes bitcoin the first to be bought by a new investor. The competing networks of Bitcoin, such as Bitcoin Cash and Bitcoin SV, are plagued by a lack of interest from serious developers, miners, and buyers. That means these networks will not be competitive with bitcoin soon. This will continue to give strength to the network spawned by Bitcoin, and the copycats do not have any hope.

THE ETHEREUM NETWORK: THE WINDOWS OS OF THE '90S

The Ethereum network is a world computer. A decentralized processing unit (DPU) facilitates the execution of computer code in a decentralized manner. The code forms the basis of smart contracts that encode conditions and value distribution in the network using cryptocurrencies.

Programmers create smart contract applications on top of the Ethereum network, which are known as dApps. For example, decentralized applications in the space of DeFi (decentralized finance) are Uniswap, a decentralized exchange, and Compound, a money-market protocol for lending and borrowing. The more dApps are added to the Ethereum network, the stronger the network effect becomes.

"Ethereum's network effect derives from developers who deploy apps—each becomes a building block that other devs can compose into higher-order services, driving increased usage and demand for ETH," wrote Jesse Walden in his article on Andreessen Horowitz.

Remember, in the late '80s, Microsoft OS was the dominant operating system. Microsoft OS achieved dominance by attracting many application developers and creating product ecology with IBM and others. Similarly, Ethereum has come to dominate the ecosystem of smart contract platforms, even though there are serious issues with traffic congestion and high gas prices on the Ethereum network. As long as the dApps built on top of the Ethereum network stay, it will remain in the lead.

Ethereum's lead should not be taken for granted, though.

Robert Leshner, CEO of Compound Labs and creator of Compound protocol, said at the DeFi Summit, REDeFiNE TOMORROW, "Ethereum, the network upon which most DeFi projects are built, may no longer be up to the task. Ethereum has high composability, but it is slow and expensive to use and reaching its limitations. An unfortunate consequence of this would be it is no longer economically viable to use for smaller transactions and users."

As we will see in the next chapter, many companies and products become victims of their success. They are unable to serve smaller transactions and users with niche needs. This allows a more agile player to capture that overlooked segment and move up the value chain, ultimately capturing the incumbent's market. A phenomenon is known as disruptive innovation.

THE FINANCIAL ANALYST'S DILEMMA

As discussed in previous chapters, the financial analyst lacks tools to value products and companies with increasing marginal returns. The primary characteristic of many new economy companies and blockchain protocols is the network effect. As seen in this chapter, the network effects can help products create and capture markets in unexpected ways. An inferior product like MS-DOS replaced the dominant OS CP/M, which was similar in functionality. MS-DOS also took the lead over Apple's Mac OS. This outcome of the OS wars is difficult to predict using standard economic and financial models.

The products that spawn networks can see exponential growth in their userbase to a varying degree depending on how the network scores on various characteristics. **A new product, marginally superior to the existing product that initially created the network, can capture the network leaving the incumbent to bite the dust.** If an analyst only focused on the accounting statements of such a company, she would completely miss the unstable nature of the market equilibrium of its products.

Blockchain protocols are decentralized in nature, which means networks are at the core of their foundation. Everything we discussed about the networks in this chapter is relevant to analyzing these protocols and their associated cryptocurrencies. Ignoring this fundamental aspect of public blockchain has led many in the financial industry astray. They have continued to apply old tools of analysis which provide an incomplete picture of these protocols' value. Additionally, these old valuations and financial analysis tools do not consider the network properties these protocols spawn, leading to incorrect assumptions about the competition and resilience of these protocols to provide long-term value.

In the next chapter, we will build our understanding of the network-based new economy and look deeper into the inherently unstable nature of products and firms in such an economy through the prism of disruptive innovation. This will help answer questions like: Which smart contract platform will succeed in the future? Will bitcoin continue to maintain its lead?

CHAPTER 10

Disruptive Innovation

"Success is never final, and failure is never fatal."

—WINSTON CHURCHILL

Will bitcoin be the world's reserve currency, or will another nimbler and more advanced cryptocurrency take its place? Will Ethereum provide the foundation of decentralized applications (dApps) that will create Web 3.0, or will the faster and cheaper Solana take its place? These questions are on everyone's mind in the crypto community. They are critical for an investor who wishes to bet on the future of these projects.

Matthew Hougan, CIO of Bitwise Asset Management, a Cryptocurrency Index Fund provider, said, "I think people who anchor on the idea of crypto as a currency reflexively dismiss it because they know 'this time is different' are the four most important, expensive words in the English language." Matt added, "A new Internet currency falling from the sky is something we've never seen before. People who view it instead as a core technological breakthrough that allows money to move over the Internet have seen this movie dozens of times. Every time we figure out how to do something on the Internet, it creates a massive disruptive industry. Figuring out how to send mail over the Internet disrupted the Postal Service. When people figured out how to do telephony over the Internet—AT&T has never been the same, right?"

Disruption is the name of the game in the early stages of foundational technology. Public blockchains are going through the same ebbs and flows. One needs to understand how disruption happened in other high-tech economies and then draw lessons to decide how the cryptocurrency ecosystem will evolve.

DISRUPTION IN PLAIN SIGHT

Founded in 2012, Coinbase facilitates the trading of bitcoin and other cryptocurrencies, most of which have not existed for more than a decade. On October 21, 2021, at the current market cap of sixty-three billion dollars, Coinbase is valued more than the New York Stock Exchange (NYSE), Chicago Mercantile Exchange, Intercontinental Exchange, and every other exchange in the United States you can name.

The New York Stock Exchange started in 1817 and had a total of more than thirty trillion dollars of securities traded in 2020 alone. It is valued at close to twelve billion dollars. Will Coinbase one day expand into trading tokenized securities and dethrone the incumbents like the NYSE?

SUSTAINING INNOVATION: A WINNER'S CURSE

In an article on innovation, "Disruptive Technologies: Catching the Wave," Harvard Business School professors

Joseph L. Bower and Clayton M. Christensen identify why leading companies often fail to stay at the top of their industries when markets and technologies change. The most fundamental reason is this they stay close to their customers (Bower et al. 1995).

The leaders often fail because they do all the things the textbook ordered. They only innovate to bring incremental benefits to their most demanding customers to keep ahead in the game and the competitors at bay. Clayton Christensen calls these innovations that make good products better in the eyes of their existing customers "sustaining." For example, a better TV picture, an additional blade in a razor, or a sleeker iPhone may be due to incremental advances or breakthroughs. Still, they are made to improve the experience of their most profitable customers.

When making decisions about investment in new technology or product, the managers look at their existing customers and evaluate whether they will value the product to make the company's investment profitable. This approach often blinds the companies to the needs of low-end customers or future customers as they align themselves tightly around their existing customers.

DISRUPTIVE INNOVATION: INCUMBENT'S NEMESIS

Christensen defines "disruption" as a process whereby a smaller company with fewer resources is able to successfully challenge established incumbent businesses.

Incumbents focusing on their most demanding customers try to exceed these customers' needs, who are also the most profitable. This focus ignores the needs of low-end customers for whom the incumbent's product is too feature-rich and expensive. Entrants can target those overlooked segments by delivering the functionality required by this segment at a lower price. By targeting the low-end segment of the market, the entrant gets a foothold in the market.

Given the entrant focuses on a segment of the market unimportant to the incumbent, the entrant does not face pushback. Entrants then move upmarket, often delivering the mainstream customers' desired performance and attributes using sustaining innovation through rapid technological growth while preserving their initial advantage. When mainstream customers start using entrants' products in volume, disruption occurs.

The entrants keep the low-cost advantage, which creates margin pressure on the incumbents who require a high margin to sustain their high-cost base.

THE BLOCKBUSTERFLIX

Netflix was founded by Reed Hastings and Marc Randolph in 1997 during the dot-com boom. Like many entrepreneurs of the time, the duo wanted to start a dot-com business and agreed to try mailing DVDs for a monthly subscription fee.

The movie rental business was dominated by Blockbuster, a household name and large company with over sixty thousand employees and nine thousand stores across the United States. Blockbuster customers were impulsive movie lovers who watched the latest releases. On the other hand, Netflix DVDs took several days to arrive by mail. Its customers were online enthusiasts and movie buffs who didn't mind waiting. It was a small, low-end segment and underserved market Netflix captured quickly. Netflix's subscription-based model brought stable revenue, helping it grow. Also, in the late '90s, anything with a dot-com in its name and a stable revenue was a hot investment.

To bring in new subscribers, Netflix gave the first month free, as that would allow the subscribers to get comfortable with Netflix's new website and rental process. This meant Netflix had an upfront customer acquisition cost. Netflix would recover this cost from the customers over the next twelve months when they started to pay for Netflix's services. At the height of the dot-com boom, if you were burning cash but increasing the userbase, you were valued highly by Silicon Valley and would not have trouble raising cash from investors.

This all came crashing down in March 2000 when the dot-com bubble burst. Netflix was in a fifty-million-dollar debt and needed cash to add new subscribers. After the bubble burst, the investors in dot-com companies got burned badly and the days when a net cash flow-negative company could raise vast sums of money were over. "Orders are flying in, but the money is flying out faster," said Marc Randolph in a retrospective interview. "We are going to go bankrupt being successful."

Reed and Randolph decided to do what any business in their position would: reach out to a larger competitor who could buy them out. After several unsuccessful attempts, they were invited to fly to Dallas to meet Blockbuster management. According to Marc, the meeting was going well until they were asked how much they wanted for Netflix. When Reed asked for fifty million dollars, essentially their debt, things went downhill.

"They basically laughed at us," Marc said, "at the hubris this company that was on the upside-down balance sheet, the peak of the dot-com bubble collapsing and dot-com on their name, had the hubris to ask fifty million dollars for their struggling company.

"It was an extremely sobering moment. And I remember thinking there was no easy way out. There was no trick. There was no gimmick. We would have to take this head-on. And it galvanized us that we would have to fight our way through Blockbuster.

"And it's an interesting story because the company Blockbuster could have purchased for fifty million dollars in 2000 now has a market cap of 250 billion dollars. And this company, which used to have sixty thousand employees and nine thousand stores, is now down to one store left, which also doubles up as an Airbnb."

Blockbuster made a blunder, but hindsight is twenty-twenty. At the time, Blockbuster was a very successful company with large operations around the United States. Its mainstream customers did not want to wait for a DVD to arrive in the mail. It did not make sense for Blockbuster to pay large sums of money for a company whose small target segment was made of movie buffs and online nerds.

Blockbuster did what the management gurus had ordered. It ignored a low-end, low-margin segment that was not its core focus.

In Marc's words, "If you're the six-billion-dollar corporation, there is a totally different moral in that story, which is about innovation and disruption. And if you're unwilling to disrupt yourself, you're just leaving yourself wide open for someone else to do it to you."

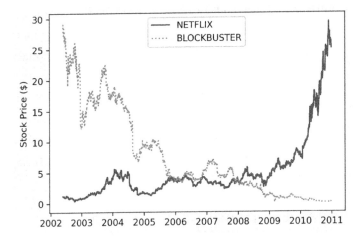

Blockbuster and Netflix Stock Price 2003–2011

In another path to disruption, entrants create new markets where none existed—by turning nonconsumers into consumers.

In the 1970s, Xerox was the leader of photocopiers, which catered to large corporations. Xerox needed to charge high premiums to provide the services large customers required. By successfully satisfying its primary customers' needs, Xerox ignored the needs of small businesses and libraries involving carbon paper and mimeograph machines.

In the late '70s, new entrants introduced low-cost, small-sized personal copiers that satisfied this overlooked segment's needs, creating a new market in the process. Ultimately, firms like Canon became significant players in the mainstream market Xerox targeted.

When small players like Canon brought personal copiers to the market, their throughput was too slow to attract large corporations. Canon did not directly challenge Xerox, so it experimented, learned, improved, and survived. Canon's small size also gave it the agility to fail fast and retry. Once it captured the lower end of the market, it had built enough experience and heft to move upmarket through sustaining innovations and bringing its copiers' performance to par with the Xerox machines while keeping its low-cost, low-size advantage. As its products became competitive in Xerox's customer segment, it started capturing market share from Xerox (Bower et al. 1995).

HOW TO BOIL A FROG

Alfred F. Kelly, Jr. is CEO of Visa Inc., a leading global payment solutions company that facilitates electronic fund transfers throughout the world. In September 2018, when asked in a club luncheon at Boston College Chief Executives Club about Bitcoin and blockchain, Kelly said, "It's an interesting technology. It isn't really at its core, for us, a good technology" (Ryan, 2018).

According to Kelly, Visa was far ahead of Bitcoin and blockchain when it came to the number of transactions per second, as its payment networks had a capacity of sixty-five thousand transactions per second. It had seventeen thousand employees, out of which were about 250 PhDs who did research, and about 840 employees were fully devoted to cybersecurity. Visa's market cap is more than four hundred billion dollars, and it has grown twofold since the beginning of 2016.

It seems Visa is doing all the right things. Its heavy investment in research and cybersecurity is to make the merchants and customers feel secure while using their Visa cards. In reality,

Visa seems to be following a pattern of how leaders in various sectors have been disrupted.

Visa is a global behemoth that, with a few other payment solution providers such as Mastercard, has no perceptible new competition. It provides a valuable service to customers and merchants around the world but at a very high cost, as it has to pay for a large workforce that develops and maintains its technology. It further uses the legacy financial system organized by a global mishmash of outdated and cumbersome technologies, rules, and regulations that make it expensive for Visa to provide its services.

When Kelly talks up the number of transactions per second his network can handle, he is simply talking about the number his network can record. These transactions get settled through the financial system, which takes much longer. It may take merchants several days to receive their money. Merchants also need to save valuable customer information in their databases, which is always a lucrative target for hackers.

Think of the last time you got a refund through your credit card. How long did it take for the money to arrive in your account? Think of how your credit card experience has changed over the past decade—probably not much. You still pay a high fee for small transactions. Your card gets blocked every time your purchase pattern deviates from your "regular" pattern. The risk someone will use your card without your permission remains high.

Visa continues to do sustaining innovation in improving cybersecurity, which is an outcome of the way its business provides payment services. The disparate nature of intermediaries and the need to save customer-specific information in multiple places managed by these intermediaries outside the Visa network makes all of them a potential target when a hacker wishes to steal customers' information and money.

In contrast to Visa, Bitcoin has no employees, as its network is managed in a free and open manner by scores of volunteers around the world. Additionally, its mining process allows miners who are independent of Bitcoin to keep the network running. Bitcoin is a decentralized payment system with no need for financial intermediaries. The security and accounting features that introduce enormous costs in Visa's business are automatic to the Bitcoin protocol and require no additional effort.

Bitcoin came from nowhere in 2009, and its market cap has gone from six billion dollars in early 2016 to more than one trillion dollars in October 2021. In other words, it is now more than twice the market cap of Visa, and it has grown about 100 times as compared to twofold growth in Visa's market cap. Bitcoin has settled more than ten trillion dollars in the transaction since its inception twelve years ago, out of which about 8.5 trillion dollars was settled on the Bitcoin network in the past three years.

Visa is a business and Bitcoin is a foundational technology like the Internet. If Bitcoin continues its upward trajectory, which is very likely, Visa's current payments business will be disrupted. By that time, the proverbial water will be too hot for Visa to react, just like a frog in boiling water.

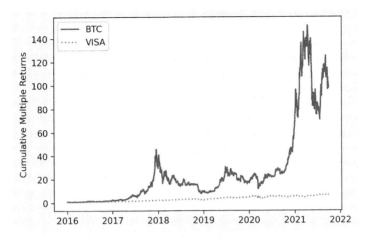

Cumulative Multiple Returns (the Value of an Initial Investment of One Currency Unit) of Bitcoin (BTC) and Visa

BACK TO THE FUTURE

It is hard to predict which disruptive innovations will survive in the long run. **As a foundational technology develops, the disruptors themselves get disrupted as they find themselves in a similar situation to those they had disrupted.**

Products like Microsoft's MS-DOS which can lock in markets using network effects are more likely to succeed. Others in the blockchain space who embrace old models such as exchanges, OTC brokers, and asset managers will face stiff competition, as they can't lock in markets without network effects.

At present, Coinbase is a clear winner when it comes to building services for a foundational technology the old-timers like NYSE missed. But it may have become too much like its counterparts in the traditional world of finance and may not have the type of network effect a decentralized exchange can create.

The rise of DeFi should come as serious competition to the centralized exchanges in cryptocurrencies. Uniswap, a decentralized exchange that allows token holders to swap their tokens without going through a centralized intermediary like Coinbase, has grown exponentially in just one year. From a minuscule volume in July 2020, it traded more than ten billion dollars per month in cryptocurrencies by October 2021. The fee accrued from the trading on this exchange goes to those holding Uniswap's governance token, UNI, which has risen to number thirteen on the list of cryptocurrencies ranked by market cap. The current market cap of UNI is more than thirteen billion dollars. Notice it is already higher than the valuation of NYSE.

Coinbase will also be forced into sustaining innovations to keep its current crop of customers happy, which could be the institutional investors, at the expense of potentially disruptive innovation, which is already happening on DeFi platforms like Uniswap. Only time will tell whether Coinbase remains on the top. But one thing is clear: Bitcoin and DeFi protocols are positioned to take over the financial technology (fintech) space.

As Mike Novogratz told me, "Crypto at its core is macro. It's about predicting the future. It's about social and economic trends."

PART 4

THE FINANCIAL ANALYST

Valuation is a core step in investing. This section will teach how traditional financial analysis tools need to be recalibrated for analyzing cryptocurrencies—a high-growth, start-up-type, equity-like investment.

By the end of this section, you will learn:

- To differentiate between the investment approaches of Wall Street and Silicon Valley.

- A step-by-step valuation exercise showing how to value a tech start-up.

- How to apply the technique developed for the valuation of tech start-ups to cryptocurrencies.

CHAPTER 11

A Tech Déjà Vu

———

"The future is already here—it's just not very evenly distributed."

—WILLIAM GIBSON

Technology investing does not only require a different set of analytical tools, but also a different mindset. Many technology products exhibit increasing marginal returns due to network effects. Furthermore, it is often difficult to predict technological breakthroughs in advance. The fields of economics and finance are rooted in the study of products and firms, which exhibits an equilibrium state of competition, products, and prices. Such economic systems are relatively well understood, forming the core of economic theory and financial analysis.

The NASDAQ crash in 2001 must have come as a relief to the investors who ignored the dot-com boom as irrational exuberance. But the next two decades would not be so kind to them. Two investors, Warren Buffett and Marc Andreessen, clearly show this dichotomy. Warren Buffett is a legendary investor in old economy companies who in 2008 became the wealthiest person in the world.

The performance of technology stocks dominates the first two decades of this millennium. In 2001, technology companies such as Amazon, Google, and Netflix were left for dead by the investors. They would be derided for the next several years by many investors such as Warren Buffett. These investors preferred the stability and predictability of the old economy companies such as banks, consumer staples, and automobiles.

Marc Andreessen, on the other hand, is a techie who built the first Internet browser, Netscape, which kickstarted the Internet. The success of Netscape was short-lived, though. The first network on the Internet created by Netscape was quickly gobbled up by Microsoft, which used its monopoly position of the Windows operating system to push its browser, Internet Explorer, to all PCs using Windows OS. Marc will continue to invest in the technology of the future. Founded in 2009, his firm Andreessen Horowitz, also known as a16z, became a leader in tech investing in under a decade. The firm became an early investor in Facebook, Twitter, Bitcoin, MakerDAO, and a large number of cryptocurrency projects which would shape the future of the technology industry for the next several decades.

A16z invested several billions of dollars of its investors' money in blockchain and cryptocurrency projects.

Right at its beginning, a16z invested in some of the great tech successes, including Facebook, Foursquare, GitHub, Pinterest, and Twitter. The firm started with three hundred million dollars in capital, and by 2012, it had over 2.7 billion dollars in assets under management (AUM). Success as a VC gave them shiploads of money and seats in the top power structure of the most successful companies. They have a vantage point many investors can only dream of. Marc sits on the board of Facebook. He was also on the board of HP from 2008 to 2018.

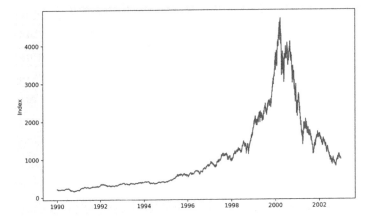

NASDAQ 100 Index 1990–2003

"WHY SOFTWARE IS EATING THE WORLD"

In a 2011 *The Wall Street Journal* essay titled "Why Software Is Eating the World," Marc Andreessen predicted, "the era of software and Internet were upon us." He said, "Over two billion people now use the broadband Internet, up from perhaps fifty million a decade ago when I was at Netscape, the company I cofounded. In the next ten years, I expect at least five billion people worldwide to own smartphones, giving every individual with such a phone instant access to the full power of the Internet, every moment of every day" (Andreessen, 2011).

The promises of software took more than two decades to be realized since the dawn of the Internet era. Software companies like Facebook and Twitter were enjoying the fruits of over six decades of research and development in the areas of telecommunications and microprocessor technology.

Memories of the dot-com crash lingered in investors' minds and made them skeptical of the billions of dollars of software companies' valuation like Facebook, Twitter, Skype, and Groupon in the private markets. Marc pointed out, "But too much of the debate is still around financial valuation as opposed to the underlying intrinsic value of the best of Silicon Valley's new companies. My own theory is we are in the middle of a dramatic and broad technological and economic shift in which software companies are poised to take over large swathes of the economy" (Andreessen, 2011).

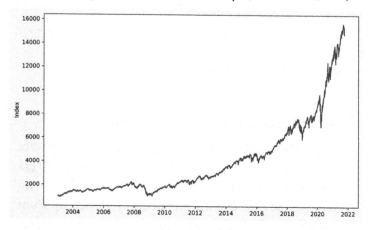

NASDAQ 100 Index 2003–2021

THE HYPE CYCLE

It should not be surprising to those who follow the evolution and growth of new technologies the Internet took such a long time to deliver on its promises. In fact, Gartner, a leader in innovations research, has developed a model popularly known as the Hype Cycle. The model uses various stages of growth to describe the growth of a breakthrough technology or innovation. In the Hype Cycle, an innovation triggers, followed by the peak of inflated expectations, the trough of disillusionment, the slope of enlightenment, and finally, it reaches the plateau of productivity (Blosch, 2018).

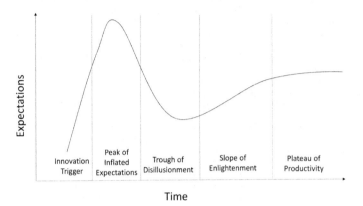

Gartner's Hype Cycle

The Netscape browser was the trigger of innovation, and the dot-com bubble and burst were the peak of inflated expectations and the trough of disillusionment respectively. With the new technology, it can be easily seen the markets and investors are often out of sync with the actual progress in the technology—an outcome likely due to herding behavior among investors.

When a new technology takes shape and shows great promise, the investors often take large risks in hopes of making large returns, sometimes to the tune of more than one hundred times. Initial investment is followed by the media, and talking heads generate inflated expectations about the technology.

Inflated expectations cause investors to herd into the technology for fear of missing out (FOMO). The FOMO investors cause steep price rises in the businesses behind the technology. This attracts more FOMO investors. The steep price rise gives early investors an exit opportunity as they achieve their target return and start selling out. This is followed by the exit of early FOMO investors, who never had any fundamental belief about the value of the technology itself.

When large numbers of investors exit and enter a market at the same time, the prices fluctuate a lot. This is also known as heightened volatility among financial players. The volatility can cause large price swings and spook the investors who can decide to exit en masse. If everyone is a seller and there are no buyers in the market, the prices will crash. This all happens almost independent of the change in the value of the technology itself.

This crash, like the one during the dot-com era, is often followed by a decade of consistent technological progress on the slope of enlightenment. In the end, technology becomes ubiquitous, but investors remain skeptical of the promise of technology due to their painful experience at the trough of disillusionment.

While leading investors, including Warren Buffett, the CEO of Berkshire Hathaway, ridiculed Facebook and Amazon, Marc Andreessen was making a case for their dominance in the next several decades. With the benefit of hindsight, we know Marc hit the bullseye with his predictions while Mr. Buffett, also known as the Oracle of Omaha, missed the major growth stories of this time by several miles.

Mr. Buffett avoided investing in the major success stories such as Amazon. In January 2020, Amazon touched the one-trillion-dollar market cap. Mr. Buffett said ruefully, "I was too dumb to realize. I did not think [Bezos] could succeed on the scale he has" (Clifford, 2019).

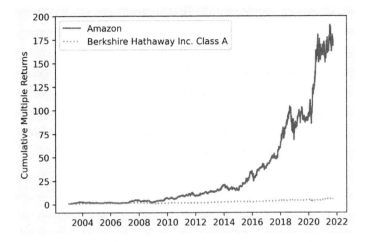

Cumulative Multiple Returns of Amazon and Berkshire Hathaway

"WHY BITCOIN MATTERS"

In 2014, Marc wrote another influential essay in *The New York Times* titled "Why Bitcoin Matters." Marc's primary insight in this essay is laid out as follows: "A mysterious new technology emerges seemingly out of nowhere, but actually, it's the result of two decades of intense research and development by nearly anonymous researchers.

"Political idealists project visions of liberation and revolution onto it. Establishment elites heap contempt and scorn on it.

"On the other hand, technologists—nerds—are transfixed by it. They see within its enormous potential and spend their nights and weekends tinkering with it."

Andreessen further adds, "Eventually, mainstream products, companies, and industries emerge to commercialize it; its effects become profound; and later, many people wonder why its powerful promise wasn't more obvious from the start."

Andreessen continued, "What technology am I talking about? Personal computers in 1975, the Internet in 1993, and—I believe—Bitcoin in 2014" (Andreessen, 2014).

The Buffett followers and many on Wall Street saw a repetition of the 2000 dot-com bubble in 2012 when upstart Internet companies like Instagram were getting valued in billions. Marc Andreessen saw the world differently and said the Internet companies had a lot more value, as they would be able to replace traditional brick-and-mortar businesses. In many cases, they would create businesses by creating services that had never existed before.

The fact of the matter is in 2000, the Internet was in the trough of disillusionment on the Hype Cycle. By 2012, it had gone up the slope of enlightenment. Later, in this decade, it created enormous wealth and value for its promoters and investors. Wall Street was simply looking at the cycle all wrong. Marc, on the other hand, was aware of how new technology evolves through various stages of the Hype Cycle and grows into a stable productive technology.

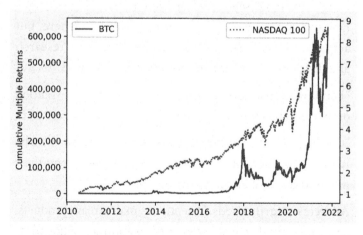

Cumulative Multiple Returns of Bitcoin (Left Y-Axis) and NASDAQ (Right Y-Axis)

EARTH USED TO BE FLAT

These two different investing paradigms are often at odds with each other. In the traditional world of finance, where close to three hundred trillion dollars of assets are managed using tools for financial analysis and valuation, the impetus is often on the predictability of cash flows. Predictability in the large swathe of the financial markets is necessary, not a criticism of this approach. Social and economic stability requires the public and institutions to make predictions and plan accordingly. **This need for predictability does not mean one should ignore a much smaller segment of high technology that has a high uncertainty associated with its future path. This segment often brings breakthroughs and advancements by solving seemingly intractable problems and changes the world for the better. A bet on this uncertainty, when successful, rewards the investor handsomely.**

The unpredictability of blockchain technology's growth and its ecosystem does not mean we should ignore the valuation and financial analysis tools honed over decades. They need to be recalibrated and used to learn as much as possible about an investment in blockchain projects. We may not predict the future, but that doesn't mean we should not evaluate it using the tools available at our disposal.

In the rest of this section, we will focus on one such tool— the valuation. In the next section, we will use what we have learned in all the previous sections and apply financial theories, such as the modern portfolio theory, which has become a cornerstone of investing, to build a portfolio of cryptocurrencies.

CHAPTER 12

A Valuation Conundrum

"Sizing the market for a disruptor based on an incumbent's market is like sizing the car industry off how many horses there were in 1910."

—AARON LEVIE

In the previous chapter, we saw some of the smartest investors, such as Warren Buffett, get the valuation of high-growth technology companies wrong. The valuation of a technology start-up is even more difficult.

Most tech start-ups do not make profits during the stages of rapid growth as they build their infrastructure and acquire new customers. Suppose the start-up is disrupting an existing industry and also expanding its boundaries. In that case, it becomes even more difficult to make any projections about demand, revenue, and profits, as the market structure is not certain. This was true of the early stages of tech companies, like Uber, and cryptocurrency, like bitcoin and ether. There was no comparable history that could help make reasonably accurate predictions about the revenue and profit of Uber and the potential market cap of bitcoin and ether.

Valuation is a key piece of any investing puzzle. How it is used can vary significantly from one use case to another. Suppose you are calculating the value of a US government bond, whose cash flows are known with (almost) complete certainty. In that case, the output of your valuation model, such as a discounted cash flow (DCF) analysis, becomes the primary basis of any investments, as your valuation must accurately reflect the bond's intrinsic value with certainty.

Suppose you are valuing the stock of a publicly traded old economy company such as ExxonMobil. In that case, you can use its financial statements, growth projections, and predictions about the global economy to arrive at a reasonable stock value. Remember, old economy companies operate under long-term stable market conditions.

Valuing a new economy company like Tesla, which is going through rapid expansion and working on battery technology and autonomous driving, becomes difficult. This is where you evaluate potential scenarios for Tesla which may deviate significantly from each other in terms of outcome and impact on company profit and stock prices.

The exercise becomes uncertain when you are valuing a tech start-up with network effects, increasing marginal returns, and an unstable market equilibrium. Here, the large variability among your scenarios leads to large variability in valuation.

In this chapter, you will look into a valuation debate about Uber. You will see how valuation tools should be used for a new economy start-up like Uber and what can happen if you incorrectly apply them. This discussion is important to cryptocurrencies, as many professional analysts have tried to use valuation approaches from mature and stable markets to value cryptos such as bitcoin and ether. In most cases, no satisfactory valuation method or value has been found, keeping most Wall Street investors in traditional markets like stocks and bonds away from cryptocurrencies.

A BATTLE OF VALUATIONS: THE ACADEMIC VS. THE PRACTITIONER

Valuation is at the core of most investment analyses. Valuation of an asset is about finding the present value of all the future cash flows from the asset. The asset's price, on the other hand, is determined by the markets when the asset changes hands between a buyer and a seller. The value and price of the asset need not be the same. This discrepancy gives rise to an investing strategy known as value investing. If an asset has a price lower than its value, then the asset is deemed to be undervalued. An investor who believes the price will rise to meet the asset's value can buy the asset and wait for value and price to converge, making a profit.

This simple and intuitive idea behind value investing is not always practical. Its applicability is limited to the assets that generate cash flows which can be determined with high certainty.

Valuation becomes difficult when the asset is a business or technology whose cash flows cannot be determined with certainty. The model still works, but the model's inputs are estimates that can be wildly inaccurate. When inputs to valuation models such as future cash flows are not certain, the value is more open to interpretation. This leads to disputes between various parties who wish to determine the value of the same asset.

In June 2013, *The Wall Street Journal* reported five-year-old car-for-hire service Uber was close to finalizing their next fundraising round of over five hundred million dollars at a valuation of seventeen billion dollars (MacMillan et al. 2014). The investment would give the investors in this round 5 percent of an equity stake in Uber. This would quadruple Uber's worth within a year. The round led to heated competition among VCs, including the venture arms of some Wall Street biggies such as BlackRock, the eight-trillion-dollar asset management behemoth. A seventeen-billion-dollar valuation would put Uber at the top of the league table of private tech companies.

The early 2010s saw large IPOs of tech companies, such as Facebook, and valuations of private tech companies, like Airbnb and Dropbox, in tens of billions of dollars. To many in Silicon Valley, this was a sweet realization of a tech dream that had once bitten the dust in the aftermath of the NAS-DAQ crash at the turn of the millennium. To the skeptics on Wall Street, this era was a repeat of the excessive and frothy valuations seen in tech stocks toward the end of the last millennium.

The sky-high valuation of tech companies looked like an anomaly to Wall Street, confirmed by their previous experience with the dot-com bubble. Uber's valuation brought out gloves on Wall Street. The leading voice behind the opponents of the Uber valuation was Aswath Damodaran, the New York University professor of finance whose extensive work on research and teaching valuations have given him the nickname "the Dean of Valuation."

Damodaran wrote a scathing article, "Uber Isn't Worth $17 Billion," about Uber's valuation on FiveThirtyEight, a respectable, data-driven news and analysis website owned by ESPN's sports network. In this article, Damodaran provided a step-by-step numerical calculation showing why Uber should be worth far less than its current valuation by the VCs.

A private company does not need to publish its financials to the public. Additionally, the information about the company's strategic plans, products, markets, and competitive landscape is often available only to the VCs, who are bound by some type of nondisclosure agreement. In sum, the primary inputs to a valuation model are not publicly available, and an analyst needs to scour through media articles about the company and interviews of the managers and investors to create a narrative about the company. This narrative helps in estimating various inputs to the valuation model.

In a simplified valuation analysis, an analyst goes through the following steps:

Estimate Revenue

1. Estimate the potential market size in terms of annual revenue for the company's products. This market size is known as the total addressable market (TAM).

2. Estimate the growth rate of this market. Using this growth rate, you can make forecasts about TAM.

3. Find out how the competition will affect a company's share of the market and estimate its market share (MS).

4. Multiplying TAM and MS, obtain company's revenue for several years in future.

Calculate Profit

1. Estimate the company's expenses in operating its business and any investments needed.

2. Calculate profit for the next several years by reducing revenue by expenses each year. Apply tax rates to find posttax profit for each year.

Estimate Value

1. Use a discount rate that reflects the risk of investing in the company to calculate the present value (PV) of future cash flows.

2. Add the value of the company's assets to the PV.

TAM and MS are the most challenging part of the estimation. Once an analyst has determined the markets and users of a company's products, other inputs such as operating expenses, tax, discount rates, and reinvestment needs are known with relative ease and certainty. For this reason, we are going to focus on TAM and MS in the discussion below.

DAMODARAN'S ANALYSIS

In obtaining the TAM of Uber, Damodaran assumed "the primary market Uber is targeting is the taxi and limo service market globally." Using the size of the taxi and limo businesses from major economies, Damodaran arrived at a TAM of one hundred billion dollars and a growth rate of 6 percent over the next decade. Using the TAM and growth rate, Damodaran projected the TAM for the next ten years (Damodaran, 2014).

Damodaran argued governments would continue to control the local taxi markets, keeping it splintered. The regulation would, of course, make it difficult for Uber to expand the market. He estimated a market share for Uber of 10 percent.

Using a TAM of one hundred billion dollars, a growth rate in TAM of 6 percent, and Uber's market share at 10 percent, Damodaran projected Uber's revenue for the next ten years. Making reasonable assumptions about operating costs, tax, and discount rate for Uber, he determined the profits and arrived at the future cash flows of Uber. Applying a discounted cash flow (DCF) model, he estimated Uber's value at 5.9 billion dollars.

DCF

To understand DCF, let's walk through a simple example.

If you put one hundred dollars in your savings account, which pays you 10 percent annual interest, you calculate the future value (FV) of one hundred dollars in one year as:

100 dollars + 100 dollars * 10 percent = 100 dollars*(1+10/100) = 100 dollars*1.1 = 110 dollars.

Now let's say you expect to receive 110 dollars in one year. What is the present value (PV) of this amount?

PV (value today of 110 dollars received in one year) = 110 dollars/(1+10/100) = 110 dollars/1.1 = 100 dollars.

As you might have guessed, PV is just backward from FV, which is also known as compounding. In PV calculations, instead of going forward in time, you are going backward.

BACK TO DAMODARAN

Damodaran understood his assumptions that Uber was targeting the global car-for-hire market might not be accurate. He developed various scenarios in which Uber would have different TAM and MS from the base case to account for this uncertainty.

According to his model, Damodaran found Uber would need to have a significantly larger TAM or MS to reach a potential valuation of seventeen billion dollars. In Damodaran's view, these scenarios were unlikely to happen in Uber's case. He concluded his article by saying, "The list of Uber's investors includes some of the biggest names in venture capital, and you may be tempted to conclude, given their pedigree, they must know something we don't. You may be right, but I wouldn't be that quick to conclude smart investors always make smart investment judgments."

BILL GURLEY RESPONDS

Less than one month later, on the morning of July 11, 2014, Damodaran sat at the Vienna International Airport waiting for a connecting flight to his home in New York. He received an email from Bill Gurley, the managing partner of the top Silicon Valley VC firm Benchmark.

A VC firm raises money from investors and then puts that money to work by investing in early-stage start-ups, hoping to win big when they scale and are listed on a stock exchange in an IPO.

Bill essentially gave Damodaran a heads-up as a volley of punches was coming Damodaran's way in a rebuttal to his article in FiveThirtyEight (Gurley, 2014). Damodaran did not know Bill personally, so the email came as a surprise to him. For the next few hours, Damodaran would get messages from the readers of Gurley's post asking for his response. Damodaran read the post and started a valuation debate that would last well into the next decade.

Damodaran's valuation of 5.9 billion dollars for Uber implied Benchmark and other investors in the latest funding round of Uber had overpaid by about 200 percent. This was bad news for the investors in Uber for two reasons. Firstly, the investors in Benchmark's fund would be very unhappy paying this kind of premium. Secondly, Damodaran's analysis suggested

Uber would have to reduce its valuation at the time of a potential IPO, leading to losses for Uber's current investors.

Talking about Damodaran's valuation of Uber, Bill Gurley said, "Using a combination of market data, math, and financial analysis, Professor Damodaran concluded his best estimate of the value of Uber is 5.9 billion dollars, far short of the value recently determined by the market. This estimate of value was tied to certain 'assumptions' with respect to TAM (total addressable market) as well as Uber's market share within that TAM. And as you would expect, his answer is critically dependent on these two assumptions" (Gurley, 2014).

TOTAL ADDRESSABLE MARKET (TAM) ANALYSIS

In his analysis, Gurley drives directly into the heart of Damodaran's arguments. Damodaran assumed a service like Uber would have no impact on the TAM of the car-for-hire transportation market. Even though Damodaran considered the possibility Uber may have some network benefits, he concluded those scenarios were improbable in Uber's case. According to Damodaran, the network Uber eschewed was weak compared to a social media network like Facebook, which meant Uber would not have a winner-takes-all outcome of other tech companies with a stronger network.

Gurley argued that was short-sighted and based on the assumption the future would be like the past. Uber's services were making radically different offerings to its customers compared to the car-for-hire transportation market. A few of Uber's benefits over the traditional market it was targeting were obvious. Uber, based on an app, improved the pick-up times and coverage density. Mobile-based payment, the dual-rating system, and the ability to track the cars all enhance users' experience—these enhanced experiences would increase the propensity of customers to hitch a ride with Uber in suburban areas, provide an alternative to rental cars, and supplement mass transit.

I had personally used more Uber rides in suburbs than I would have taxis before Uber. Suburban taxis were far less available, often dirty, and unreliable. I would only use a taxi on rare occasions. I can see Gurley's argument that Uber has significantly expanded the limo and taxi services market.

The game-changer, though, would be Uber as an alternative to car ownership. Gurley said, "Damodaran likely never considered this possibility: could Uber reach a point in terms of price and convenience it becomes a preferable alternative to owning a car?" (Gurley, 2014)

According to an American Automobile Association (AAA) estimate, the average cost of car ownership in the US is nine thousand dollars per year. If you divide that number by your average Uber fare, you can estimate how many Uber rides you can have by replacing your car. You may find there are far too many rides you do not need.

According to several news articles published in *The Atlantic*, *The New York Times*, and *Time* during the early years of Uber, young Americans were doing just that—ditching their cars.

In 2014, the number of cars on the roads in the world was over one billion. The United States accounts for 25 percent of the global car market. Assuming a conservative estimate of the average cost of car ownership of six thousand dollars per year, instead of the original nine thousand dollars, Gurley arrived at a market size of six trillion dollars (one billion cars * six thousand dollars per car), which Uber-like services could potentially disrupt. Gurley further assumed that Uber-like services could capture 2.5 to 12.5 percent of the total car market as an alternative to car ownership. This would add a further 150 to 750 billion dollars to the market size based on a six-trillion-dollar car ownership market.

Uber's market share in San Francisco at the time of Gurley's writing was already three times the original taxi and limo market. This clearly showed Uber was already expanding the market. Given this was still the early stages of Uber, Gurley assumed Uber would expand the original market by three to six times, which would mean a market size of three to six hundred billion dollars based on the initial market size of one hundred billion dollars.

The two market sizes would range from 450 billion to 1.35 trillion dollars based on the above calculations. Compare that to the total market size of one hundred billion dollars estimated by Damodaran, who did not consider the possibilities Uber would disrupt the taxi and limo markets and expand the market multifold by disrupting the car ownership market.

The TAM range of 450 billion to 1.35 trillion dollars would ultimately be shared by Uber and its competitors. Even though Uber was kicking off the market, its share would drop as others saw the lucrative opportunity and jumped into the fray. This is exactly what happened, as Lyft, Didi, and Ola were started worldwide to challenge Uber's position in these markets.

MARKET SHARE (MS) ANALYSIS

Damodaran estimated Uber's maximum market share at 10 percent, citing regulatory restrictions and competition.

Disagreeing with that number, Gurley wrote, "Is Uber exposed to some form of network effect where the marginal user sees higher utility precisely because of the number of previous customers who have chosen to use it, and would that lead to a market share well beyond the 10 percent postulated by Damodaran?" (Gurley, 2014)

Uber's service reduces the wait time for drivers and passengers. This increases resource utilization by Uber—rides per hour by the drivers—allowing Uber to lower fare prices while keeping drivers' income fixed. Reduced fare increases demand for Uber drivers and increases geographic coverage. Increased geographic coverage is a type of network effect. The network effect provides Uber with increasing marginal returns and a greater market share due to a first mover advantage.

Remember, we saw in the chapter "A Tale of Two Economies" the new economy firms have a unique first mover advantage due to network effects and increasing marginal returns. In such markets, what is bigger gets bigger, and the market often becomes a winner-take-all proposition for the first mover. In sum, Gurley was postulating Uber will become the ultimate winner in the expanded market and attain a market share of higher than 10 percent of the one-hundred-billion-dollar taxi and limo market, as postulated by Damodaran. Gurley concluded Uber's opportunity was about twenty-five times bigger than Damodaran's ten-billion-dollar estimates. At the lower TAM range of 450 billion dollars, Uber needed a market share of about 56 percent (=250/450) to achieve a 250-billion-dollar target market. At the time of Gurley's article, Uber's market share in San Francisco was already higher than that.

Damodaran took Gurley's critique in stride and revalued Uber at close to fifty-four billion dollars. Five years later, Uber went public at a valuation of 75.5 billion dollars. Benchmark's investment of twelve million dollars turned into seven billion dollars in profits.

The final valuation of Uber was more than twelve times larger than Damodaran's and one-third of Gurley's.

So, who won?

THE WINNER

The point of the valuation debate was not to choose a winner because there can be no winners in such a debate. As we know, a high-growth tech company's valuation is difficult and uncertain at best. No matter what you value a company at, your valuation will most likely be off.

In Uber's case, Gurley's objective was not to arrive at a correct value of Uber, rather a ballpark estimate. A ballpark estimate tells investors to invest in the company today at low enough prices, so there is a high margin inbuilt into the deal. This margin is the price of the uncertainty the investor is charging. It does not matter whether Uber's final valuation at the time of IPO and most likely exit point for VC from that investment came close to the initial estimate. What is important, though, is the final value was high enough to make it a worthwhile investment. That was possible due to the high margin.

As we saw in Uber's example, the traditional Wall Street approach to valuation is not applicable for technology like Bitcoin, which has network effects and increasing marginal returns. To value bitcoin and other cryptocurrencies, you need to understand they are highly disruptive technologies with network effects of varying strengths. You need to create your estimates of cryptocurrency value by creating narratives. You create the alternative narratives or scenarios using your knowledge of the technologies (Section Two) and how the crypto will expand the historical market shares. How will old and new firms be disrupted by the fast-developing technology and product ecosystem (Section Three)?

Accuracy is the key for valuation models on Wall Street, which often plays on a lower margin of errors. It uses a large amount of capital to generate returns from investments in the debt and equity of stable and mature businesses.

By applying a heavy discount to the value obtained through the valuation analysis, VCs allows for a large margin of error.

WHERE DO WE GO FROM HERE?

You can't predict the growth of the technology sector with confidence. The changes in technology can bring fundamental changes traditional economic and financial analysis tools can't capture. A cool marketing campaign for Coke has a predictable impact on its market share and future revenue. On the other hand, advancements in semiconductor technology can fundamentally alter the capabilities of handheld devices like smartphones. Who could have predicted by the year 2020, the number of people accessing the Internet from their phones would be 4.3 billion, rising from zero in 2006 (Johnson, 2021)? The impact of such capability and smartphone penetration has led to trillion-dollar companies such as Facebook and Netflix.

If you can't correctly predict the impact of changes in technology on a firm's product or industry, you would not get accurate valuations for that firm. This chapter looks at the valuations from the traditional perspective of Wall Street analysts and not-so-traditional approaches taken by Silicon Valley investors. In the next chapter, you will see how a legendary Wall Street investor, Bill Miller, approached the valuation of bitcoin in a method more akin to a VC investor and became one of the rare Wall Street investors to buy bitcoin at less than three hundred dollars.

CHAPTER 13

Valuation of Cryptocurrencies

———

"Price is what you pay; value is what you get."

—BENJAMIN GRAHAM

Crypto networks, such as Bitcoin do not have any cash flows. Their primary purpose is a peer-to-peer payment currency network. In the absence of any current or future cash flows, the value of bitcoin will be determined by demand and supply, like commodities. This demand will be driven by potential use cases of bitcoin such as a medium of exchange and store of value.

Smart contract platforms, such as Ethereum, provide services to decentralized applications (dApps) like DeFi protocols. Ether is used for gas-fee in smart contract executions. The demand for ether is driven by the demand for smart contracts on the Ethereum blockchain.

DeFi governance tokens can accrue transaction fees and commissions and have more clearly defined revenue models.

In each case, one can value an underlying cryptocurrency by using some comparable. For example, you can look at what product or service a cryptocurrency project is replacing, then use the value of that product or service as a potential value for the cryptocurrency project. The replacement value approach will not give an upper bound on the value, as it does not consider the effects of lower transaction costs and network properties. These may further expand the original markets as Uber did by expanding the geographical reach for a car-for-hire market and unexpectedly partially replacing the car ownership market. If you can identify these effects, you can potentially find a higher expected return in your cryptocurrency investments.

You can obtain the potential return by using the current price of the crypto as an initial investment and the value you get through your valuation exercise as the future price, then calculating the percentage change between the two. The higher the potential return, the higher the margin in the investment and the larger your position in that investment can be. This is particularly important when you are trying to construct a portfolio of traditional assets and cryptocurrencies.

BILL MILLER: A VALUE INVESTOR'S CASE FOR BITCOIN

According to Bill Miller, the legendary Wall Street investor, value investing is often generalized to investing in assets with low accounting multiples—for example, assets with a low-price-to-earnings ratio. Miller takes a broader approach that accepts the past is not necessarily representative of the future, which can evolve in multiple scenarios with different probabilities. **Suppose we can determine the values of an asset in each of these scenarios along with the probabilities**

with which each scenario will be realized. In that case, we can determine the expected value of the asset by taking the weighted average value, using probabilities as weights.

The use of expected value is ubiquitous in finance. However, it is not much used in valuations, but in other areas, such as trading, options pricing, and risk management, finding expected value of assets and portfolios is a core exercise. To illustrate this point, let's see how stock options are typically valued. An option on a stock is derivative security, whose future payoff is contingent on the price of the stock. Since no one has a crystal ball to see what the future price of the stock will be, the analysts identify all potential price scenarios of the stock, calculates the option payoff, and then takes the weighted average of all these payoffs where weights are the probabilities of each scenario being actually realized. **A probability-weighted average is obtained by multiplying payoffs by their probabilities, summing these multiples, and then dividing by the total of the weights.**

Bill Miller, a value investor in the veins of Warren Buffett, took an early interest in bitcoin when the rest of Wall Street was goading in the pernicious light bitcoin found itself in after the hack of the largest cryptocurrency exchange, Mt. Gox, in February 2014 when 850 thousand bitcoins were stolen (Miller et al. 2015). The hack followed the shutdown of the notorious website Silk Road, run by Ross Ulbricht, who ran a drug empire on the dark web under the pseudonym "Dread Pirate Roberts."

I was among the majority of the Wall Street professionals who believed bitcoin was an anonymous currency used by drug traffickers and would be ultimately banned by the government. This was and remains a pervasive view among

Wall Street professionals too busy to learn about a fringe technology that pretends to unseat the king of all currencies, the US dollar. Unfortunately, almost everything said or argued about the detractors of cryptocurrency at that time and now comes from a misunderstanding of the technology and its potential.

There is also a noisy set of Bitcoin proponents who are in an incessant debate about how Bitcoin would dethrone the whole financial system. These proponents, also known as Bitcoin maximalists, argue ad nauseam with those who disagree with their views. The public at large is a spectator to this conversation and ends up making conclusions about bitcoin based on arguments that may have no relevance. Remember Bitcoin is decentralized, which means it does not have a CEO or public relations department, so anyone with a loud enough voice can act like the chief media relations officer of Bitcoin.

These great debaters, though, provide fodder to cynics and proponents alike. During its early years, a majority of people on Wall Street took in the ready-made views of these debaters and concluded it was a passing fad.

Narratives are important. To identify potential scenarios, you have to build narratives based on your understanding of the asset and the economy it is part of. If you choose a wrong narrative—which among professionals is often an outcome of biases, prejudices, or conflicts of interests—you might assign incorrect probabilities. For example, those who thought it was a matter of time before the governments shut down Bitcoin in 2014 had assigned a near-zero probability to any scenario in which Bitcoin would succeed. Assigning nonzero probabilities to multiple scenarios requires diligence, hard work, and of course, a desire to derive an expected value from these future scenarios. As you saw in Uber's case, your valuations depend on the narratives you create or adopt. The trick is to build as many narratives as possible and assign probabilities to the individual narratives. By taking a weighted average value, you arrive at a ballpark figure, which should help you determine whether an asset is undervalued and by how much. This should allow you to decide to invest in this asset irrespective of the stage of growth of the asset.

Miller's narrative about bitcoin in the September 2015 article stands on two pillars. The first one identifies the negligible transaction fee in the Bitcoin network compared to the traditional payment networks like Visa and Mastercard, which charge the greater of 3 percent and fifteen cents. According to this narrative, the low transaction fee of the Bitcoin network makes it much cheaper than a traditional payment network. I couldn't agree more with the Millers. Sending Mother's Day gifts to my mom in India has cost me more than what the best flowers would cost because the banks and payment networks used their oligopoly to charge large transaction fees for international remittances. People accept these fees and costs as a matter of fate and carry on with their lives. With Bitcoin, this can significantly change. On the other hand, micropayments can expand new markets to low-price, low-margin goods and services, similar to how Uber expanded the car-for-hire market by providing a car ownership alternative. Given bitcoin is a digital native, this can release enormous economic activities on the Internet.

The second narrative builds upon bitcoin's fixed supply managed by computer code. Bitcoin, as we know, is also decentralized, so no individual or entity can unilaterally decide to increase the number of total possible coins. This is in contrast to sovereign currencies, where central banks around the world have been playing God by printing enormous amounts of sovereign currencies. The federal reserve in the United States alone added more than three trillion dollars over a few months in 2020, almost 20 percent of all money in circulation in the United States. All of this money supply can create inflation and debase US dollars, as there will be too many dollars chasing the same assets. In simple terms, your savings in dollars will be worth much less in the future. Not surprising if you believe in gravity and the law of supply and demand.

The decentralized nature of the network and Bitcoin's fixed supply make it an attractive store of value asset. Bitcoin, in fact, is even better than gold, which has been used as a store of value for thousands of years. As the digital native millennials and Gen Z come of age, it is likely they will choose a weightless, almost infinitely divisible, instantly transmissible digital alternative to gold bars.

As Mike Novogratz pointed out, "The tribalism we see in crypto helps define what bitcoin did. It created this idea you could have a digital store of value, a digital community that gets together and imbues value into something."

Miller writes, "We use the aforementioned background as a starting point for a valuation case. The technological breakthroughs, security, low transaction costs, and decentralized nature of the system all mean no one knows how valuable the system may become. However, if adoption grows, so should its aggregate value as a payment system. A growing system value, measured by the market capitalization of bitcoin, should mean a growing value of bitcoin given the limited supply of the denominator."

The reduced cost of transaction takes market share from the existing payment networks and expands new markets in the economic activities that require micropayments.

FROM NARRATIVES TO NUMBERS

Miller said, "The grandest dream for bitcoin would be for it to achieve the store of value status of gold." The total value of gold ever mined—at the spot price of 1,133 dollars per troy ounce at the time of Miller's letter—was 6.4 trillion dollars. If bitcoin completely replaced gold by the time its supply hit the maximum of twenty-one million dollars in the year 2134, every bitcoin will be worth about 314 thousand dollars. Miller concludes this is a highly unlikely scenario and assigns it a small chance of 0.25 percent.

In the payment processing narrative of bitcoin, it may replace the payment processors like Visa, Mastercard, and American Express. Their total market capitalization at the time was 315 billion dollars. If bitcoin captured this value, then at the maximum supply, each would be worth seventeen thousand dollars. Per Miller, "This is still unlikely, but more likely than the value-reserve status of gold." They assigned the payment processor replacement scenario a chance of 2.5 percent.

The probabilities need to sum to one or 100 percent once all the potential scenarios are considered.

According to Miller, the third extremely likely scenario is bitcoin does nothing, i.e., it turns worthless. They assign the rest of the probability of 97.25 percent to this particular scenario. This was still an early phase of bitcoin.

As per Miller's estimates, the expected value of bitcoin is as follows:

Numerator (sum of value multiplied by their respective probabilities) = 315,000 dollars * 0.25 percent + 17,000 dollars *2.5 percent + 0 dollars*97.25 percent = 1,212.5 dollars.

Denominator (sum of weights) = 0.25 percent + 2.5 percent + 97.25 percent = 100 percent.

Expected value = Numerator/Denominator = 1,212.50 dollars.

At the time of the analysis, bitcoin was trading at 230 dollars, meaning bitcoin's expected value at the time was more than five-fold. Miller's decision to invest in bitcoin, as their calculation showed even considering the high probability the bitcoin would become nothing, had a steep potential upside—a perfect value trade. There was a huge margin of safety built in this investment.

This sounds exciting but can be disturbing as well. To many investors, a 97.25 percent chance of losing all their investment will sound reckless, no matter the expected return. However, this is where portfolio construction comes into the picture, which will be thoroughly covered in Part Four.

The difference between Gurley's valuation of Uber and Miller's valuation of bitcoin is Miller assigns probabilities to scenario-based values, whereas Gurley only provided a range. One approach is not necessarily better than the other. However, arriving at reasonable probabilities is a complex task. Given the uncertainty in the final valuation, it should not matter whether your valuation is in a range, like Gurley's, or a single expected value, like Miller's.

VALUATION OF BITCOIN IN PRESENT

Many valuation methodologies of bitcoin have been proposed. They all have one thing in common: the final valuations are inherently uncertain. Given this uncertainty, it is safer to use simple and intuitive models. Miller's model uses probabilities, which may be difficult to calculate. Instead, one can use a range of values by finding the minimum and maximum value using various narratives. An approach we take in the following section.

In the first chapter, Damodaran said bitcoin was most likely a currency. According to research by Geoff Kendrick, head of foreign exchange research at Standard Chartered, a British multinational banking giant, bitcoin shares characteristics with currencies, commodities, and equities in early-stage tech companies.

BANKING THE UNBANKED

There are about 1.7 billion unbanked people in the world. You will be surprised to know, according to a survey by the Federal Deposit Insurance Corporation (FDIC), over 6 percent of US households—which is a total of fourteen million adults— are unbanked. In the chapter on disruptive innovations, we saw the new entrants often start by serving an overlooked segment of a market. The incumbents focus on the needs of their current and most profitable customers while ignoring the lower end of the segment. With banks, it is the cost of servicing the customers—including identity management, recording and storing transactions, providing statements, and compliance—which make it prohibitively expensive to serve the needs of smaller customers, leaving behind a large segment of the population outside the banking system.

Bitcoin is an open-to-all peer-to-peer payment system. According to the World Bank, the unbanked population could account for twenty trillion dollars of annual transactions. To open an account, buy and use bitcoin, all you need is a mobile phone. About half of the unbanked already own a mobile phone. Geoff's team estimates that if bitcoin captures all of the twenty-trillion-dollar transactions, its market cap would be one trillion dollars. This estimate is based on comparables using the payment processors such as Visa, Mastercard, and American Express, which handle twenty trillion dollars in transactions and have a total market cap of about one trillion dollars. The total eventual supply of bitcoin will be 21 million in 2140. If we divide one trillion dollars by twenty-one million, we get a bitcoin value of about fifty thousand dollars (Kendrick et al. 2021).

THE STORE OF VALUE

Limited supply is the primary property of a store of value. A currency or commodity that does not have an upper limit to its supply cannot act as a store of value. For example, the total supply of gold is limited by how much gold is under and above ground. A sovereign currency like the US dollar, which is not backed by any commodity, is printed by the government and has a potentially infinite supply. The US central bank has printed several trillion dollars since 2008. As seen in Chapter Two, the size of the Federal Reserve balance sheet stood at about nine hundred billion dollars in 2008, rising to close to 8.5 trillion dollars by October 2021.

New bitcoins are minted by the miners with every new block added to the blockchain. Fifty bitcoins were minted with the first block mined by Satoshi. The total supply of bitcoins is capped at twenty-one million. So, the rate of new bitcoin supply, which is bitcoin mined with each new block, has to adjust downward with time. This adjustment has happened about every four and half years at a predetermined block number, which is encoded in the algorithm. The first halving to 25 bitcoins happened in 2012, the second to 12.5 bitcoins in 2016, and the third to 6.25 bitcoins in May 2020. The halving had significant upward pressure on bitcoin price, as can be seen in the chart. The next halving will take place sometime in 2024.

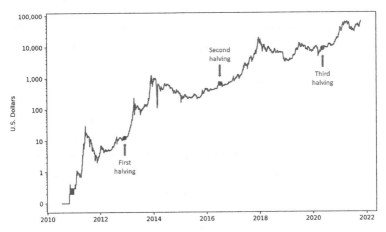

Bitcoin Price (Log Scale) and Halving

The miners compete to solve a computation puzzle to win the lottery of adding a new block to the blockchain. The miners earn a reward in newly minted bitcoin and the transaction fee associated with the transactions added with new blocks. The difficulty of the computational puzzle is adjusted so that, on average, a new block on the bitcoin blockchain is added roughly every ten minutes. If several computational units deployed by miners rise, a measure known as hash rate rises. The algorithm will adjust the puzzle's difficulty upward to account for a higher hash rate. If the hash rate goes down, as when China recently banned all miners from the mainland, the hash rate went down and difficulty adjusted downward.

The last bitcoin will be mined in the year 2140. Afterward, the miners will earn only the transaction fee associated with the transactions added with new blocks. The finite supply of bitcoins and its current low inflation rate of 1.8 percent per year, compared to a normal growth rate of 5 percent of the US M2 money supply, gives an inflation rate differential between bitcoin and the US dollar. The inflation rate differential means the total number of bitcoins is growing much slower than the money supply in the United States, making bitcoins more expensive when measured in US dollars. Based on these inflation rate differentials, a fifty-thousand-dollar price of bitcoin today will equal 120 thousand dollars in 2140.

The two narratives, the payment processing for the unbanked and store of value, give bitcoin a valuation of 170 thousand dollars (50 thousand dollars +120 thousand dollars). Based on the above discussion, the minimum value of bitcoin would be 50 thousand dollars if the store of value scenario for bitcoin failed to realize. The maximum value would be 170 thousand dollars if bitcoin realized both scenarios.

PRICING THE END GAME

Geoff said, "The financial markets tend to price the endgame." The endgame of bitcoin is it becoming the medium of exchange for the 1.7 billion unbanked and replacing gold as a store of value. Even though these events will happen in the future, the markets will price them much earlier. So, you will not have to wait until the year 2140 to see the last bitcoin mined to capture the return associated with bitcoin becoming a less volatile store of value and a medium of exchange.

VOLATILITY DEBATE

One primary concern about bitcoin used as a store of value and medium of exchange is its volatility. Bitcoin volatility is about five to ten times higher than gold, S&P 500, and a highly volatile emerging market currency such as the Turkish lira (TRY). The bitcoin prices have been trending upward since the beginning, and volatility has come down. The high bitcoin price volatility stems from the long-term investors who wish to extract long-term returns from bitcoin. This holding pattern has led to a lack of liquidity in the market, causing price swings. As bitcoin prices approach their long-term value, these holders will no longer need their bitcoins. This should increase liquidity and reduce volatility closer to the level of major sovereign currencies, making it a suitable medium of exchange and store of value.

PORTFOLIO FLOWS AS AN ALTERNATIVE VALUATION MEASURE

Bitcoin has a low correlation with traditional assets like stocks and bonds. Given the high returns throughout its history, bitcoin significantly enhances a traditional 60/40 portfolio's (60 percent stock and 40 percent bond) risk-adjusted returns or Sharpe ratio, as we will see in a later chapter. Many academic papers have been published recommending a 2 to 5 percent allocation to bitcoin in an investor portfolio.

At current prices, the market cap of gold (ten trillion dollars), global equities (ninety trillion dollars), and global fixed income (280 trillion dollars) lead to a total market cap of traditional investment assets at 380 trillion dollars. The bitcoin market cap at present is about one trillion dollars, which means it can rise to 7.6 trillion dollars (2 percent of 380 trillion dollars) when 2 percent of the global market cap of all traditional assets is allocated to bitcoin, giving approximately a seven-fold increase in the price of bitcoin. Let's make a conservative estimate of five times from fifty thousand dollars and value bitcoin at 250 thousand dollars in this use case (Kendrick et al. 2021).

VALUING A SMART CONTRACT PLATFORM: ETHEREUM

Ethereum is a smart contract platform and can support many aspects of finance like borrowing and lending, insurance, and exchanges. Ethereum smart contracts are not limited to DeFi. According to ConsenSys, a company owned by cofounder of Ethereum Joseph Lubin, smart contract platforms can be used to disrupt the supply chain, law, Internet of Things, and many other industries. Within the blockchain space, Ethereum has been successfully used for ICO (Initial coin offerings), smart contracts, decentralized finance (DeFi), decentralized autonomous organizations (DAOs), NFTs (nonfungible tokens), and stablecoins.

We will primarily focus on the DeFi aspect of Ethereum. Still, you can use these ideas to include more scenarios where Ethereum and dApps built on Ethereum can capture market share from other industries and expand these markets' sizes.

First, notice the difference between Ethereum and Bitcoin. Bitcoin is a peer-to-peer payment system with a native currency, bitcoin. Bitcoin is often referred to as "digital gold." Ethereum, on the other hand, is an infrastructure, a world computer on which decentralized applications are built. Ether is the native currency of this platform, used to initiate transactions and execute smart contracts. Ether is often referred to as "digital oil," which propels the economy on the Ethereum platform.

SUPPLY OF ETHER

Unlike bitcoin, the total supply of ether is not capped. Instead, there is a limit on the annual issuance of ether. Also, Ethereum has a strong community led by its cofounder, Vitalik Buterin. Even though the governance of Ethereum is somewhat decentralized, Vitalik has a strong voice and a large number of followers. That is both good and bad. The good part is Ethereum can adjust to software bugs, traffic congestion, and gas pricing to improve the network performance and usability. The bad part, though, is decision-making is not as decentralized as it is for Bitcoin.

To value ether, Geoff's team used approaches similar to bitcoin. In one approach, they looked at the share of existing markets Ethereum could capture and did a relative valuation based on what incumbent firms holding that market share were valued at.

ETH VALUATION USING METHOD OF COMPARABLES

If we focus only on the DeFi use case, Ethereum is to global banks what Bitcoin is to the credit card companies. The market cap of global banks is about four times the market cap of credit card companies. This makes the potential market cap of ether four trillion dollars (the market cap of global credit card companies is one trillion dollars). There is about 117 million ether currently outstanding, which gives a value of thirty-five thousand dollars to ether, roughly tenfold from the current price level.

ETH VALUATION USING SIZE OF THE PORTFOLIO FLOWS

As we saw before, the size of the crypto markets can grow to about 7.5 trillion dollars simply to accommodate a 2 percent portfolio allocation to crypto. Ether has been the second-largest cryptocurrency after bitcoin for several years. Ethereum has a large number of use cases compared to Bitcoin, and the ether market cap could likely grow to be as large as bitcoin. This means the 7.5-trillion-dollar market cap would be divided between these two and other more niche cryptocurrencies such as governance tokens of DeFi. Bitcoin dominance among all cryptocurrencies has hovered around 66 percent. If ether and bitcoin have the same market cap and their total dominance remains at the long-term bitcoin dominance of 66 percent, ether will have a 33-percent market share. This gives ether a market cap of 2.5 trillion dollars (33 percent of 7.5-trillion-dollar total crypto market cap). Divide this number by total ether outstanding (currently 117 million) and you get a value of 21,500 dollars, which is five to six times from current price levels (Kendrick et al. 2021).

VALUING DEFI GOVERNANCE TOKENS

You can use the method of comparables to estimate the value of DeFi governance tokens. Many governance tokens accrue fees and commissions earned by the platform. This should give you the revenue of the platform. You can use revenue multiples to find the value of various governance tokens.

By now, you should have a good grasp of how to value cryptocurrencies. To summarize, here are the steps:

1. Identify the use cases of the cryptocurrency and the underlying value proposition. For example, in the case of Bitcoin, it was "facilitating a peer-to-peer currency system." In Ethereum's case, it was a smart contract platform that provides infrastructure for decentralized finance.

2. Find incumbent comparables in the nonblockchain world. For Bitcoin, these were the payment processors like Visa, Mastercard, and American Express. In Ethereum's case, these were the financial institutions.

3. Estimate how much of the market the platform can capture from incumbents. For Bitcoin, this was the potential transactions from the unbanked, and for Ethereum, it was the banks.

4. Using token economics within the blockchain network, estimate the value of each cryptocurrency.

Once you develop narratives about the future path of a crypto project, you can apply a valuation technique similar to those used in this chapter.

You can compare the present price of the cryptocurrency underlying the project to the value you calculated and identify if there is sufficient margin that makes the cryptocurrency an attractive investment. In venture capital, you are looking at least a three to sixfold return depending on your time horizon.

Before you can invest in the selected cryptocurrencies, you need to figure out how much of your wealth should be in crypto and how much you should invest in each cryptocurrency. The next section digs into these issues.

PART 5

THE INVESTOR

This section is about how to select and invest in crypto-currencies. The knowledge you have developed in previous sections using various hats—the historian, the technologist, the venture capital analyst, and the financial analyst—now culminates into you, the investor.

By the end of this section, you will learn:

- How to evaluate cryptocurrencies.
- How to create a portfolio of cryptocurrencies.
- A crypto strategy showing large returns compared to bitcoin.

CHAPTER 14

The Crypto Opportunity

___

"It's about time!"

—GUY ON GREEN, *HAPPY GILMORE*

If you are a cryptocurrency coin picker (like a stock picker), your approach to crypto is more like a VC. If you like to trade or actively manage your risk, you are more like a Wall Street investor.

Notwithstanding what type of crypto investor you are, you will need to apply the tools of both types. Cryptocurrencies share the risk-reward characteristics of early-stage start-ups and the liquidity profile of stocks. If your approach focuses on one and ignores the other, you are either taking more risk than you should or leaving money on the table. Most likely, it is both.

While driving through the guts of crypto technology and valuation in previous sections, you may have noticed the focus was more on a venture investment type of analysis. This section brings in Wall Street to enhance the value generated by a VC approach to cryptocurrencies.

The Wall Street investor has the benefit of many securities getting traded in each asset class. The trading history of these securities, including price and volume information, allows one to gain a deeper understanding of the asset class structure, such as the division of securities in sectors. As we will see in later chapters, such an approach provides diversification and enhances risk-adjusted returns. The risk-adjusted return is also an important measure of investment; the higher, the better. It allows an investor to compare the performance of different investments. Is an investment in Tesla better than bitcoin, or vice versa? It also allows for a quantitative approach to adding new assets to your portfolio.

Cryptocurrencies are also large in number and have a trading history like stocks and FX, albeit a shorter one.

CORE PLATFORM VS. APPLICATION LAYER

It is essential to understand at least two layers of value are captured in the blockchains—one at the core layer, the platform level, and the other at the application level. For example, you can invest in Ethereum, the base layer, on top of which other applications like Compound are built. In the Ethereum ecosystem, ether provides market beta, while Compound also provides the idiosyncratic risks associated with Compound.

In the foundational predecessor technologies such as the Internet, no tradable unit of value existed that would give investors exposure to the Internet itself. You could only get portfolio exposure to individual companies such as Amazon, Webvan, Pet.com, Netflix, etc. However, this would introduce large, idiosyncratic risks into your portfolio.

We are talking about the early growth of the Internet. In the early phases, many companies like the dot-com grocery store, Webvan, and dot-com pet supplies retailer, Pet.com did not survive, costing investors a lot of money. On the other hand, **core platform blockchains have a native asset, such as bitcoin and ether, which gives exposure to their whole ecosystem.** So, if you invest in ether, you benefit when any individual application or company built on top of the Ethereum is successful. This is because these applications need to use ether to execute smart contracts. As they become successful, the demand for ether also goes up, driving its value higher.

DISSECTING THE ECOSYSTEM

Investing in ether gives a systematic exposure to the Ethereum ecosystem. Investors can also add individual companies built on top of Ethereum to express their views on individual applications—for example, adding Compound and MakerDAO governance tokens, COMP and MKR.

In fact, the blockchain technologies' foundational nature means there are and will be several competitors in each use case, creating sectors. For example, the Ethereum ecosystem has a decentralized finance (DeFi) sector in which different companies and projects provide financial services, such as borrowing and lending, insurance, etc. Another sector on Ethereum network is Web 3.0, in which projects like Chainlink provide infrastructure to Web 3.0 protocols and projects.

We already see such sectors developing in this space from their price action. The recent price history shows that within-sector projects have a high correlation in prices and cross-sector projects have a lower correlation in prices. This provides investors with additional flexibility in customizing their exposure to the blockchain space.

DIVERSIFICATION IS KEY TO SURVIVAL

The reader should remember the blockchain space is an ecosystem of start-ups traded publicly like stocks. To make correct investment decisions, you need to use a different approach from both the venture capitalists who are start-up investors and Wall Street investors who focus on public markets such as equities.

It is quite common for investors in the blockchain space to approach the market from two directions as mutually exclusive. They do not realize this market is at the intersection of both, leading to suboptimal portfolio returns or, worse, larger-than-necessary losses.

Over the past decade of cryptocurrencies, there have been stories of great winnings and losses.

On the one hand, investors like Mike Novogratz have strategically positioned themselves in the blockchain space and have made billions over the last seven years. Mike currently runs Galaxy Digital, which is a key player in the blockchain. Over the years, Mike has invested in the base layer currencies such as bitcoin and ether, the second layer applications through their tokens, directly in the start-ups in this space, and by having a stake in Galaxy Digital.

On the other hand, Masayoshi Son, the founder of SoftBank Group, a Japanese multinational conglomerate, runs a one-hundred-billion-dollar technology fund called Vision Fund. Son bought a large stash of bitcoins in late 2017 when the market peaked at about twenty thousand dollars. He sold out in early 2018 when bitcoin plummeted by more than 80 percent. According to a *The Wall Street Journal* report, Son lost about 130 million dollars from this investment (Levy, 2019).

Others like Anthony "Pomp" Pompliano have invested about 80 percent of their wealth in bitcoin. Many of the early bulls in cryptocurrency investments continue to hold a large number of bitcoins, as seen by the hodl reports (Li, 2020).

The long-term holding investment gives the investors exposure akin to a venture capital investment. This approach completely ignores the important, underlying characteristic of being liquid. Another important aspect of venture capital is you need to invest in a large number of projects or start-ups.

HOW VENTURE CAPITAL FIRMS SUCCEED

Venture capital is a game of chance. More than 80 percent of start-ups fail within the first two years. An investor in an early-stage start-up needs to invest in many opportunities and hope a few will succeed, making up for the rest of their losses. If you distribute your capital in twenty start-ups, you hope one or two will give you ten to twentyfold returns, and a few will recover their investments. Venture capital investment is locked in, and these investments are not liquid.

Venture capital investors focus on deal flow. They look at many potential investment opportunities in the start-up space. Given many start-ups do not have a proven business model, the founders' pedigree and people backing a start-up become important.

For example, Coinbase was founded by the alumni of Airbnb and Goldman Sachs in 2012. At the time, Bitcoin was only three years old. It was an unproven technology, albeit with a high potential upside. They raised money from well-known technology investors such as Union Square Ventures, Andreessen Horowitz, and Ribbit Capital.

The early backing of well-known Silicon Valley names gave Coinbase a big head start against rivals, and it later raised significant capital from big investors to fund its breakneck growth.

Coinbase investors diversified their bets by investing in several cryptocurrency start-ups. Their bet was to invest in many companies in this space, so they end up getting a few big hitters. The big hitters would compensate these investors for the losses in the failed ventures.

HOW WALL STREET INVESTORS SUCCEED

On the other hand, investors in public equities can rebalance their portfolios among a universe of public and often liquid stocks. These investors' objective is to maximize returns for a level of risk they have accepted. They do not need to be worried the companies in their portfolio will not make it, as the bankruptcy of publicly traded companies is not that common. Rather, their focus is maximizing their risk-adjusted returns—that is, for a given level of risk the investor is willing to take, the returns are maximized.

In addition to returns, the investors in public markets are also focused on the liquidity and risk of their investments. This also leads to the concept of active risk management applied by these investors. They do a valuation of their portfolio holdings regularly, even daily, and calculate their portfolios' profit and loss (P&L). Risk management by these investors is focused on making losses stay within acceptable limits. If and when these limits are breached, investors decide to reduce their positions or exit the investment completely.

As opposed to venture capital investors, the institutional investors in the public markets have predetermined risk limits monitored and managed by professional risk managers.

HOW YOU NEED TO BE BOTH TO SUCCEED INVESTING IN CRYPTOCURRENCIES

VENTURE CAPITAL

The venture capital's time horizon is often fixed beforehand and can vary between two to ten years. In publicly traded stocks, the time horizon could be as short as a millisecond. The point is the stock investor can react to the events surrounding the market and companies due to the liquidity.

The liquidity of crypto markets allows the investors to rebalance their portfolios and actively manage their risk. Even though the investment is still in the start-ups, they can use various active strategies, such as sector rotation, momentum, etc., to enhance their returns.

The rebalancing ability will allow crypto investors to harvest returns from this asset class's high volatility due to its low correlation with the traditional assets.

HOW A VENTURE CAPITAL SHOULD INVEST IN CRYPTO

The liquid nature of many cryptocurrencies that allows an investor to calculate their profit and losses (P&L) in an almost instantaneous manner introduces more quirks in this asset class compared to a typical venture capital investment, where the investors do infrequent portfolio valuation. In fact, the only times a fair value of their investments can be calculated is when a new investment is made in the start-up, something that can take years from the last funding round.

The liquid nature of cryptocurrencies makes it possible for any investor to actively manage their risk. A typical venture capital portfolio is made up of investments in start-ups, most of which fail. According to the Small Business Administration

(SBA), the failure rate of start-ups is more than 90 percent. This means roughly nine out of ten companies in a venture capital portfolio will fail. These failures often lead to a complete loss of capital for the investors.

Cryptocurrencies allow the investors to sell out of the investments behind the projects that aren't going well and rotate into the ones doing better. This type of active approach can significantly improve the portfolio performance, as the investor can increase the success rate of the companies in their portfolio. Additionally, they will have a much higher recovery rate in the failed projects, as the investor is able to sell their crypto holdings in the failing project long before it goes to zero.

The advent of DeFi provides attractive yield farming opportunities to traders and investors in cryptocurrencies. The long-term holders of cryptocurrencies should take advantage of earning additional yield on their holdings by lending and staking opportunities offered by centralized institutions, such as Genesis and BlockFi, and decentralized platforms, such as MakerDAO, Compound, and Aave.

Most importantly, liquidity is both the bane and boon for venture capital and hodler portfolios. On the one hand, it allows them open access to successful projects as opposed to the traditional VC sector, where the best opportunities go to a select few VC firms at the top of the food chain. On the other hand, instant liquidity makes it difficult to ignore the fluctuations in the value of their portfolios. Traditionally, a VC will raise a fund and then allocate capital across various projects. The fund will have a well-defined time horizon, which means the VC will not need to revalue their portfolio until a liquidity event happens, which are few and far between.

HEDGING AFTER MARKET RALLIES

The derivatives market has grown significantly. CME Group, Deribit, and FTX Trading Limited provide alternatives to the investors looking to hedge gains in their portfolios. The crypto market often makes significant gains only to lead to substantial drawdowns. In the past ten years, bitcoin has seen more than **four drawdowns of more than 50 percent, with a few being close to 80 percent.** Long-term investors should look into using options strategies such as buying puts or collars to protect their gains and reduce drawdown. The impact of even small reductions in drawdown could be significant.

Venture capital investors and long-term holders should also diversify their holdings across sectors of cryptocurrencies. It is likely some of the metrics applied to the hedge fund managers will be applied to the venture investors as well.

When investing in crypto, the investors need to understand the volatility introduces additional risk compared to a venture capital investment. In venture capital, an investor is locked in until the next funding round, which means they cannot react to the start-ups' valuation fluctuations. In crypto's case, the investor may exit the investment if it loses more money than the investor is comfortable with. The Nobel laureates Daniel Kahneman and Amos Tversky found losses loom larger than the gains for investors (Kahneman, 1979).

THE PROSPECT THEORY AND MASAYOSHI SON

Masayoshi Son is an exceptional technology investor. He has access to the best advice when he needs it. In fact, it was Pete Briger, the cochairman of Fortress Investment Group, a highly successful hedge fund, who recommended Son buy bitcoin in late 2017. Son invested about seven hundred million dollars in bitcoin but sold it at a 130-million-dollar loss a few months later. Even if he bought at the peak price of about twenty thousand dollars per bitcoin, Son could have made more than 175 percent returns had he stayed in the position for two more years when bitcoin price hit more than sixty thousand dollars. This would also have been within the normal fluctuations of bitcoin, as the price has shown to be cyclical in nature. It often peaks after the halving event, which happens roughly every 4.5 years.

Anthony Pompliano follows a lottery strategy, albeit an expensive one. Anthony may make an extraordinary amount of money if bitcoin continues its uptrend. However, the risk-adjusted returns would be lower than other well-diversified crypto strategies, as we will see in the next chapter.

There is no denying the cap on the total number of bitcoins that will ever be minted satisfies an important requirement for it to be a store of value. There are other issues, though. First of all, bitcoin is extremely volatile. This means there could be a significant mismatch between the time horizon of the investor liabilities and the bitcoin returns. One primary purpose of investments is asset-liability matching. If your portfolio has high volatility, which is the case with a portfolio that invests 80 percent in bitcoin, your asset-liability mismatch will be large and frequent.

Bitcoin may also lose ground to other cryptocurrencies such as ether in the future. If one looks at the computer markets in the '70s and '80s, it is not hard to see how fast the new technology incumbents got disrupted by the challengers. In the early stages of foundational technology, it is extremely hard to predict which protocol, formula, standard, or product will dominate.

The network effects and increasing marginal returns lead to a winner-take-all outcome. However, that happens when the foundations have been stabilized. By the late '90s, the Internet had stabilized somewhat. This gave Internet companies like Amazon, Netflix, and Facebook the opportunity to grow in a relatively stable environment.

In the next chapter, we will look at analyzing individual projects for inclusion in one's portfolio.

CHAPTER 15

Analyzing the Cryptocurrencies

———

"Only when the tide goes out do you discover who's been swimming naked."

—WARREN BUFFETT

There are sixty-six hundred cryptocurrencies on the website CoinMarketCap.com. Unlike stocks, which give you equity in publicly traded mature companies, cryptocurrencies are easy to create. Anyone can copy open-source protocols, make minor changes, and create a protocol with a new set of cryptocurrencies. How do you determine if this project has long-term potential?

During bull markets in cryptocurrencies, investors often indulge in speculative cryptocurrency buying based on their price action without any rational analysis about why that cryptocurrency should be in the investor portfolio. People justify their decisions based on irrelevant information, like a celebrity endorsement. It is also possible investors end up buying quality coins based on price action. However, if the investor bought a cryptocurrency without researching, they are often not committed to the investment. This is problematic in crypto because the high volatility of cryptocurrencies means at some point, the cryptocurrency's price will show a significant downward movement. For example, a small market cap cryptocurrency has daily volatility of 5 percent. Assuming a normal distribution of returns, this means about 33 percent of the time (number of days), the cryptocurrency price will move by more than 5 percent.

A portfolio of cryptocurrencies based on research is more likely to be held by an investor when a steep drawdown happens and the investor thesis has not changed. In other words, you should only sell your coins if your thesis about the cryptocurrency has changed or you have hit a predetermined risk limit. The latter is only for active investors who are managing their portfolios instead of buying and holding coins for the long-term. In the rest of this chapter, we will build upon the previous sections and Section Three, in particular, to develop a research methodology to select cryptocurrencies.

THE VALUE DRIVERS

Bitcoin, Ethereum, and many other public blockchain platforms will prove significantly disruptive because they provide privacy, fault tolerance, and certainty in a decentralized manner. Decentralization substantially reduces the transaction costs for many use cases.

The reduction in transaction costs leads to unbundling of economic activities. The lower cost makes many of the block-chains' features attractive to a much larger population. In a manner typical of disruptive technologies, many of the products built on top of these blockchains will enter the mainstream over the next decades.

The first step in analyzing any cryptocurrency is looking at the project and the token economics from the eyes of a venture capitalist.

EVALUATING CRYPTOCURRENCIES

For every cryptocurrency, you should do the following analysis. We will take Compound Finance, a DeFi project, as an example.

THE PEDIGREE

Who are the people behind the project?

1. The Team: You can find this information on the project web page. For example, according to the Compound Labs web page, the Compound protocol was developed by a team of respectable developers and leaders with a history of successfully delivering on software start-ups. According to his LinkedIn profile, Robert Leshner, the CEO, is a University of Pennsylvania graduate who also holds a CFA charter. He is located in San Francisco. Additionally, the company has more than a dozen employees.

2. The Investors: According to Compound Labs' web page, its projects are backed by leading investors such as a16z, Bain Capital Ventures, Paradigm, and Polychain Capital.

The Takeaway: The project has a history recorded by trustworthy media outlets. It has a website. The team is respectable based on their education and past work histories. You can verify the team from media and professional networking websites such as LinkedIn. You can cross-check investors listed on the web page have invested in this project by checking another database such as Crunchbase. Some of the investors will also list their investments on their websites.

Even if all of this checks out, a sophisticated scammer can make their project look legit. **So, stay away from projects that do not have a track record.** You can use a market cap threshold to ensure you are not the first money to bite in the project. For example, a market cap of one hundred million dollars in crypto projects shows decent momentum while keeping large potential upside if the project succeeds.

Stay Away: Your friend told you about a cryptocurrency that gained 1,000 percent in the past month, but you can't find any information about the team, its location, or backers. You are walking into a scam.

CLASSIFY

What is the project looking to accomplish?

1. What are the services the platform will provide once it is completed? Crypto projects often publish this on a whitepaper you can download from their website. You can also look at the project page on CoinMarket.com or CoinGecko.com to find out details of the project. For example, the following web page provides information about the Compound protocol: https://www.coingecko.com/en/coins/compound.

2. Usually, the project should be classified under some broad sector definitions. For example, the following is a list of sectors and examples of some coins which belong to individual sectors. This list will keep growing as new sectors emerge. You can find a list of sectors on Messari.io.

Sector	Top Five Based on Market Cap (October 16, 2021)
Currencies	Bitcoin, Bitcoin Cash, Monroe, Litecoin, Stellar
Smart Contract Platform	Ethereum, Cardano, Solana, Polkadot, Terra
DeFi	Uniswap, PancakeSwap, Aave, Maker, Amp
Exchange Tokens	BNB, Uniswap, FTX Token, Unus Sed Leo, SushiSwap
Gaming	Axie Infinity, Enjin Coin, The Sandbox, Illuvium, Alice
Web 3.0	Chainlink, Filecoin, Theta Network, The Graph, Stacks

Top Coins in Cryptocurrency Sectors

THE VALUE DRIVERS

Understand the drivers of value behind the project and its cryptocurrencies.

1. Identify the network properties. (Refer to Chapter Nine.)

   a. Strength of Network: Is the network the project will be embedded in solid or weak? For example, Compound has a weaker network than Bitcoin, as another DeFi protocol can quickly capture its market share by improving the protocol. This is a property of the network, not a weakness of the Compound protocol.

   b. Clustering in the Network: Is the network clustered? For example, Compound is quite popular and has a global userbase, so it is not clustered.

   c. Bridging of Multiple Networks: Can this network bridge with other networks and expand into other verticals?

   d. Risk of Disintermediation: Compound is already a decentralized platform.

e. Vulnerability to Multihoming: Various lending protocols such as Aave and Maker provide borrowing and lending of crypto assets. Users like to compare rates across protocols to optimize their yields. So, DeFi lending and borrowing is multihoming.

2. How likely is it this platform will be disrupted? (Refer to Chapter Ten.)

   a. Is a technically superior and cheaper protocol going to disrupt this one? Note from Chapter Ten incumbents often get disrupted because they are unable to focus on the future of services and features and focus on their current customers' demand instead. Ethereum is a good example of a platform that can get disrupted by another like Solana, which solves many of Ethereum's problems. The Compound protocol can also be disrupted, as the development work has mostly ceased since the team behind Compound has moved to other projects, and Compound is supposed to be managed by a DAO.

   b. On the other hand, bitcoin is more likely to keep its leading position among various stores of value cryptocurrencies. Because a store of value depends on how many high-value investors hold an asset in their portfolio. The momentum is surely behind bitcoin.

THE VALUATION

(Refer to Chapter Thirteen)

1. Identify the use cases of the cryptocurrency.

2. Assess the total addressable market (TAM) of each use case.

3. Estimate the market share (MS) of the project for each use case.

4. Based on TAM and MS, can you estimate a value?

5. If it is an existing sector, can you do a relative valuation?

6. What was the last funding round for the project, and what was the valuation? If noted VCs like a16z invested, their typical, expected sixfold return should give you a sense of the upside to look for.

7. If you can determine estimates of value through fundamental or relative valuation, you know your investment's potential return.

PERIPHERALS

1. If code repositories, such as GitHub, for the project are available, check if the code has been regularly updated.

   a. https://github.com/orgs/compound-finance/repositories

2. Coverage by research firms, such as Delphi Digital, should increase your confidence in a project.

3. Listings on reputable exchanges, such as Binance and Coinbase, are a positive sign.

THE SHORTCUT

If, for any reason, you can't perform your research and due diligence on individual projects, then piggyback well-known VCs. For example, when a16z invested in MakerDAO's governance token, MKR, one could have bought Maker coins from the market. By doing this, you benefit from the research and due diligence done by a16z.

Caveat: Invest with respectable VCs, but make sure you are not getting in when they are getting out. Given the liquid nature of the market, VCs can silently exit their investments.

POSITION SIZING

Once you have selected the coins you wish to buy and their expected returns, it is time to construct a portfolio. It would be best if you looked at your crypto holdings as a part of your portfolio of all investments, which may include stocks and bonds. Retail traders often make the mistake of looking at stand-alone crypto returns. Suppose you had 10 percent of your portfolio invested in cryptocurrencies and crypto market tanks by 50 percent, which happens from time to time. If you look at the losses on your crypto position, you lost 50 percent, which is painful for most investors. I know of a few such investors who exited their crypto position after a significant drawdown event because they looked at their crypto holdings independently of the rest of the portfolio, only to watch the markets tear through their initial entry-level and rise multifold.

If you look at your whole portfolio, your losses in the above scenario will be much lower. For example, if you had 10 percent of your portfolio in crypto and the crypto market tanked by 50 percent, your losses would be at most 5 percent at the portfolio level, assuming the price of the other asset classes did not move, or the rest of the portfolio did well, which is often the case when you have assets in your portfolio which have a low correlation with crypto. You would likely digest these unrealized losses and let the market cycle turn in your favor. If you can't digest a 5 percent drawdown on your portfolio, then you took more risk on crypto than you should have. You can avoid this situation by following portfolio construction methods, which is the topic of the next chapter.

CHAPTER 16

Crypto in a Portfolio

___

"Diversification is the only free lunch in investing."

—HARRY MARKOWITZ

You have created a favorite list of coins you wish to invest in, or you have developed an advanced methodology that gives you a list of cryptocurrencies to invest in. Before you can buy these coins, you need to determine how much money from your investment account you should allocate to cryptocurrencies. This question is important for institutional as well as retail investors.

Most investors divide their capital across various asset classes, such as stocks, bonds, real estate, and commodities. Cryptocurrencies are a new asset class, and there is no agreement about how much one should allocate to crypto. The process, however, is well understood. One only needs to find an optimal size in crypto that enhances the return while keeping risk at a level acceptable to the investor.

Harry Markowitz, who won the Nobel Memorial Prize in Economic Sciences in 1990, developed the modern portfolio theory (MPT) studying the effects of asset risk, return, and correlation on future portfolio returns and an approach to calculate an optimal portfolio of assets. This chapter will look at the inputs to portfolio optimization, which are expected returns, volatility, and correlations. These inputs are well studied for traditional assets such as stocks and bonds, and investors have built some intuition about them. Crypto is a new asset class, so we will first look at these inputs for crypto and build an intuition about them. Later in the chapter, we will determine the size of your crypto portfolio.

"You" in this particular discussion are not you, the reader. The results we derive in this chapter and the next are baseline results that apply to the proverbial investor in the financial literature and media. This investor puts 60 percent of his money in stocks and 40 percent in bonds. These results are often treated as a baseline. They are applied to an individual based on their situation and risk tolerance. This is something only you know about yourself.

Bitcoin is the crypto asset with the largest market cap and longest price history. First, we will look at various statistics of the bitcoin price series and then extend our analysis to include more cryptocurrencies.

HIGH RETURNS

Bitcoin has given exceptionally high returns in its roughly one decade of existence. According to the first publicly verifiable trading data, which dates back to July 17, 2010, the bitcoin price was five cents. If an investor put one thousand dollars in bitcoin on July 17, it would be roughly one billion dollars in March 2021, when the bitcoin price was hovering about fifty thousand dollars.

Year	Q1	Q2	Q3	Q4	Yearly Return
2010			25.0	384.6	505.9
2011	174.5	1605.7	-68.3	-6.7	1282.6
2012	5.0	32.3	83.7	10.0	180.6
2013	587.0	4.8	45.5	467.9	5849.9
2014	-44.8	42.8	-38.9	-18.0	-60.5
2015	-23.3	8.1	-10.7	82.3	35.1
2016	-3.4	61.2	-9.3	58.4	124.0
2017	12.0	129.8	75.8	217.6	1337.5
2018	-49.9	-7.8	3.7	-44.1	-73.2
2019	10.6	163.7	-23.4	-13.1	94.1
2020	-10.9	42.5	17.9	168.8	302.4
2021	103.0	-40.4	25.1	45.6*	120.4*

Bitcoin Quarterly and Yearly Returns, July 17, 2010-October 19, 2021. Source: Quantuna.com

As shown in this table, bitcoin had positive returns in ten out of twelve years and posted triple-digit or greater returns in eight of these years. This makes bitcoin the best-performing publicly available investment opportunity of recent times.

VOLATILITY

The high returns of bitcoin have been accompanied by high volatility, as measured by the standard deviation of daily returns.

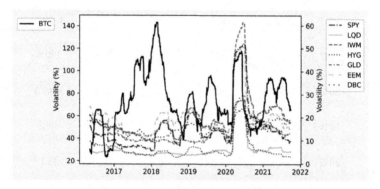

Volatility of Bitcoin (Left Y-Axis) Compared to Traditional Assets (Right Y-Axis) (Annualized 90-Day Rolling Standard Deviation), January 1, 2016-September 30, 2021

BTC—Bitcoin Spot

SPY—US Large-Cap Equities (SPY ETF)

LQD—Corporate Bonds-IG

IWM—US Small-Cap Equities (IMW ETF)

HYG—Corporate Bonds-HY (HYG ETF)

GLD—Gold Spot (GLD ETF)

EEM—Emerging Market Equities (CEW ETF)

DBC—Broad Commodities (DBC ETF)

CEW—Emerging Market Currencies (CEW ETF)

As the picture shows, the bitcoin volatility is significantly higher than the volatility of all the traditional assets included in the above picture. Volatility is used as an important risk metric in investment management. High volatility means the asset prices can fluctuate wildly, taking the investors on a roller coaster ride.

High volatility is typical of a nascent asset class that lacks a proper valuation model. If investors can't value bitcoin, then they lack an anchor bitcoin price that can be compared against. As the investor base broadens and liquidity increases, volatility should go down. Given this technology's foundational nature, we can expect the volatility to remain high for the foreseeable future.

DRAWDOWNS

High returns and volatility of bitcoin have been accompanied by significant drawdowns in bitcoin's journey. As previous table shows, bitcoin has experienced sixteen negative return quarters out of forty-five quarters since the price data is available. There are two negative return years, including 2018, when bitcoin dropped by more than 73 percent.

Large volatility and drawdowns can help investors enter the market at a lower price. They also provide more trading opportunities, as one can sell at a higher price when market is entering into a bear territory and buy back at a lower price. On the other hand, they can be quite painful for long-only investors who buy and hold the investments for a long time.

This is where investor psychology can play an important role. Even when investors know the prices will return to their uptrend in the long run, they often find it psychologically difficult to sit on large losses and may exit the investment at much lower prices. The realized loss makes it difficult for these investors to reenter the market. To avoid reacting to such drawdowns, investors need to develop narratives about why they should invest in bitcoin or any other cryptocurrencies in the first place. In addition, the investor should determine their risk tolerance and come to a level of cryptocurrency allocation they are comfortable with.

The investor should only sell out of a position if the narrative has changed. Drawdowns should affect your decision to exit a position only if they hit a predetermined loss level. However, the drawdowns in cryptocurrencies can be high, which is a direct result of high volatility and also means the market will jump back and grow higher. **So, finding a stop loss level would be very difficult and likely counterproductive.**

CORRELATION WITH TRADITIONAL ASSETS

Bitcoin has a low correlation with most of the traditional asset classes such as equities, bonds, and commodities. Bitcoin correlation with broad equity indexes such as the S&P 500 has fluctuated between -0.25 to +0.25 in the past few years.

The correlations between bitcoin and traditional assets also become high when stock markets, specifically the tech stocks, show stress. In the long-term, though, the correlations have been low.

The low correlation of bitcoin and other cryptocurrencies with the traditional asset classes makes it a great addition to a portfolio of traditional assets, as it provides diversification benefits.

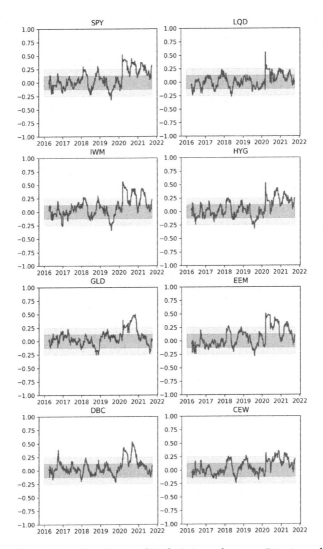

Rolling 90-Day Correlation of Daily Returns between Bitcoin and Traditional Assets, January 1, 2016-September 30, 2021

Note from the figure how the correlations between bitcoin and various traditional assets have stayed within a narrow band around zero most of the time in the past five years.

THE IMPACT OF CRYPTO ON A TRADITIONAL PORTFOLIO

A CFA Institute study showed adding bitcoin to a traditional bond (60 percent) and equity (40 percent) portfolio provides significant additional returns over the long-term on both an absolute and risk-adjusted basis (Hougan et al. 2021).

We ran our own tests to see where the Sharpe ratio would be optimal. In the graph below, we see large gains in cumulative returns as percent allocation of bitcoin goes up. The traditional portfolio is made up of 60 percent in Vanguard Total World Stock ETF (VT) and a 40 percent allocation to the Vanguard Total Bond Market (BND).

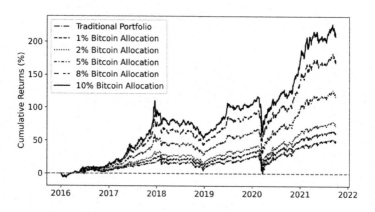

Cumulative Returns: Traditional Portfolio with and without Monthly Bitcoin Allocations, January 1, 2016–September 30, 2021. Source: Quantuna.com

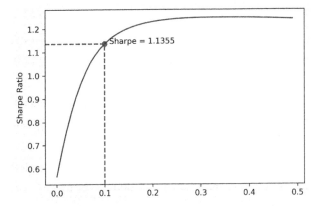

Sharpe Ratio vs. Weight of Bitcoin in the Traditional Portfolio;
Source: Quantuna.com

The large improvement in the risk-adjusted return is due to the diversification benefits of low correlation between bitcoin, stocks, and bonds. We found at a 10 percent weight of bitcoin in the traditional portfolio, the gain in Sharpe ratio (SR) starts to go down. **The Sharpe ratio is the average return earned on investment above the risk-free rate per unit volatility.**

Weight of bitcoin Percent	1	5	10	15
Annual Return Percent	8.52	14.41	21.66	28.80
Annual Volatility Percent	9.07	10.18	12.63	15.55
Sharpe Ratio	0.67	0.96	1.14	1.20
Maximum Drawdown Percent	-21.56	-22.77	-25.21	-31.93

Performance of BTC in a Traditional Portfolio;
Source: Quantuna.com

NON-BITCOIN CRYPTOASSETS

Crypto is made up of thousands of cryptocurrencies. This shows the possibilities brought about by the foundational nature of blockchain.

Bitcoin remains the dominant crypto asset with a market dominance of over 60 percent. Ethereum has consistently ranked number two for the past several years.

The total global crypto market cap is about 1.5 trillion dollars. Bitcoin alone is about one trillion dollars. Ether is about 175 billion dollars. The total crypto market cap tripling in less than a year suggests this space, as well as cryptocurrencies like bitcoin and ether, has more room to grow. In fact, some of the cryptocurrencies, such as Binance Coin (BNB), have risen more than fifty-fold within the past year during the recent bull run.

High returns of these cryptocurrencies are associated with even higher volatility and drawdowns. Investors face even more difficult portfolio management choices when it comes to these cryptocurrencies.

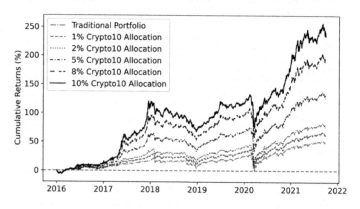

Cumulative Returns: Traditional Portfolio with and without Monthly Rebalanced Crypto 10 (Top Ten Crypto Ranked and Weighted by Market Cap) Allocations, January 1, 2016–September 30, 2021. Source: Quantuna.com

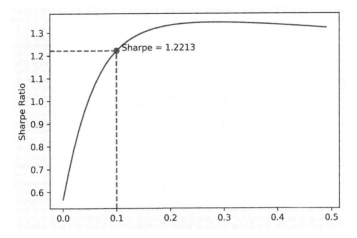

Crypto 10 in Traditional Portfolio: Optimal Sharpe Ratio;
Source: Quantuna.com

Weight of bitcoin Percent	1	5	10	15
Annual Return Percent	8.70	15.32	23.42	31.34
Annual Volatility Percent	9.09	10.18	12.55	15.38
Sharpe Ratio	0.68	1.02	1.22	1.30
Maximum Drawdown Percent	-21.63	-23.10	-25.22	-29.18

Performance of Crypto 10 in a Traditional Portfolio;
Source: Quantuna.com

SECTORS IN CRYPTOCURRENCIES

Stock investors often like to bucket stocks in sectors. Different economic sectors may respond to the expectation of the future state of the economy differently. Stock index providers MSCI and Standard & Poor's developed the global industry classification standard (GICS) for the stock markets. The GICS system divides the publicly traded stock markets into eleven sectors. The top four sectors, by their contribution to the market cap of S&P 500, are information technology, healthcare, consumer discretionary, and financials. Stock investors seek to take exposure across various sectors to reduce the idiosyncratic risk of their portfolios and enhance the risk-adjusted return.

Cryptocurrencies are not as mature as the stock markets, but cryptocurrency investors seem to follow a similar mindset as stock investors. Index fund providers such as Bitwise Asset Management have come up with Bitwise DeFi Crypto Index Fund. According to their website, "The Fund seeks to track an index of the largest decentralized finance (DeFi) crypto assets, a portfolio of protocol tokens that aspire to disrupt large parts of the legacy financial ecosystem."

Matt Hougan, CIO of Bitwise Asset Management, told me, "There's some value in thinking about subsectors where crypto might apply, having a meaningful impact, and making sure you are exposed to those subsectors."

Cryptocurrencies can be categorized into sectors based on how close their use cases are. For example, bitcoin has several companions created to solve perceived issues or add new functionalities that did not exist in bitcoin. Litecoin solves bitcoin's low transaction speed problem, and Bitcoin Cash has a large block size, allowing more transactions to be clubbed together. Monero is used by those who wish to have complete anonymity in their transactions. Similarly, there are application platforms such as Ethereum, EOS, etc. Then there are cryptocurrencies created by the exchanges, such as BNB by Binance and Huobi Coin by Huobi.

It is only a matter of time before different crypto sectors will decouple from the broad crypto markets and act differently. For example, recently, gaming- and NFT-focused cryptocurrencies such as Axie Infinity have been on a tear. Previously, the DeFi sector was going through the roof. This also shows the herding behavior of investors in various sectors, which makes it more likely the correlations between various sectors will go down and become part of any diversification strategy in cryptocurrencies.

Currently, many websites provide a category of cryptocurrencies based on their use cases. However, these categories can often run in the hundreds, which is not very useful for investment analysis. To start, you can look at the sectors identified in the previous chapter.

Armed with insights about crypto markets at a qualitative and quantitative level, we are ready to investigate a few investment strategies in the next chapter.

CHAPTER 17

Investing in Cryptocurrencies

———

"Time is your friend; impulse is your enemy."

—JOHN C. BOGLE

Once you have determined how much money you should allocate to crypto, it is time to select a strategy to invest in cryptocurrencies. This chapter discusses how a cryptocurrency picker who has a VC-type approach should invest in cryptocurrencies.

Later in the chapter, we look at a crypto strategy that is easy to implement, does not require the effort involved in VC investing, and beats bitcoin and a basket of top ten market cap weighted cryptocurrencies by a wide margin.

VENTURE CAPITAL TYPE OF LONG-TERM HOLDING PORTFOLIO

You followed the steps given in Chapter Fifteen and have a list of cryptocurrencies you wish to invest in. From the valuation exercise of Chapter Thirteen, you should also have an expected return for each cryptocurrency on your list. You can weigh each cryptocurrency in your portfolio, so the weights are proportional to its expected returns. Such weights will allow you to express your bullish views on the coins with higher expected returns. This approach does not consider the risk of individual coins. However, the overall risk you are taking on crypto is determined by the portfolio allocation exercise you did in the previous chapter.

DIVERSIFICATION

Take advantage of sectors in cryptocurrencies to provide you with an additional layer of diversification and risk control. You can bucket your coins in various sectors and then create an equally weighted basket of the sectors. You can also use a market cap weighted basket, but as we will see later, equally weighted baskets seem to perform better in cryptocurrencies.

YIELD FARMING

Once you buy the coins in your portfolio, you can further enhance returns by applying various yield farming strategies. For example, you can earn a yield on your cryptocurrencies by providing liquidity in pools on a decentralized exchange (DEX) such as Uniswap or depositing them on a lending platform like AAVE. If you want to learn more about DeFi, you can refer to a book by Prof. Campbell Harvey titled "DeFi and the Future of Finance" (Harvey, 2021).

PROTECTING YOUR GAINS

Prices of cryptocurrencies can rise manifold in a very short time. This happened especially after bitcoin halving, when every 4.5 years (roughly), miners' reward gets cut in half. This sharp price rise is often accompanied by a significant drop. As discussed in the previous section, setting stop losses could be difficult and counterproductive. Think of determining when to buy and when to sell while you are on a roller coaster ride.

Downside protection can be achieved in many other ways:

- The investor can diversify across sectors in cryptocurrencies, reducing the overall volatility of their portfolio.
- They can buy protection using cheap put options or use a collar strategy if the option premiums are high.
- They can use a trend following overlay to increase skewness—that is, increase the likelihood of large positive returns and reduce extreme downside moves.

TIMING

Instead of putting all your capital to work, you should space out your investments. The benefits are as follows:

1. Dollar-cost averaging

Given the high volatility of cryptocurrencies, the prices fluctuate wildly. The markets tend to rise sharply, especially during bullish rallies, due to increased demand from those who have a fear of missing out (FOMO) and because liquidity is often low. The low liquidity is due to long-term holdings of many large investors who do not trade their cryptocurrencies. Many new investors often warm up to cryptocurrencies in such bullish markets and end up buying at highs. They often exit the market once it settles, capturing losses and sometimes never coming back.

A better strategy to build a large position in volatile markets is to space out your buys. This is known as a dollar-cost averaging strategy, and in the long run, you will benefit by spreading your entry price over time. You will sometimes buy at highs or lows as the market fluctuates. This should lower the average entry price of your coins.

2. Opportunity to invest in new coins

It is also important to remind ourselves crypto is a nascent asset class, and new coins will continue to emerge with time. By dividing your capital across time, you will have the opportunity to invest in new coins which show promise.

REBALANCING

If your expected returns change, you should rebalance your portfolio. Suppose you invested in bitcoin and bitcoin SV. With time, bitcoin has consolidated its position as a store of value. An asset is a good store of value when a large number of investors believe it to be. Once the narrative around bitcoin as a store of value has been established, the investors will move from other competitors such as bitcoin SV to bitcoin. This means the narrative has changed, and you should reduce your exposure to bitcoin SV and instead invest that money in bitcoin.

POTENTIAL CRYPTO STRATEGIES

What if you don't have time to analyze individual crypto projects and build a VC-type portfolio? This is a common problem with a majority of investors. Index funds have been created in traditional markets to allow investors to take exposure across many underlying factors without worrying about anyone in particular. This simple approach has given good results, and research suggests index investing has beaten most of the active fund managers.

John C. Bogle simplified investing in stock markets by launching the first index fund comprised of five hundred stocks in 1976.

He founded Vanguard, which has become the most important low-cost index provider for a majority of Americans. Currently, Vanguard index funds manage about seven trillion dollars.

Bogle believed stock picking was too complex for most Americans, and a much simpler way to invest in the stock market was to hold a large diversified basket of stocks. This simple yet powerful idea has proven extremely successful, as more than half of US stock fund assets to the tune of four trillion dollars are now invested in index funds.

By investing in a large basket of stocks, the following happens:

1. You achieve diversification, which reduces overall volatility. This means drawdowns will be lower, and the detrimental effect of negative returns on the compounding is managed.

2. You are effectively taking a bet on the whole economy. If you believed in the long-term future of America in 1976, you could just hold a large basket of US stocks and not worry about picking up individual stocks.

Suppose you are convinced the public blockchain technologies, such as decentralized currency, smart contract platforms, DeFi, etc., have a great future, but you are not sure which of these thousands of projects will succeed. In that case, you can use Bogle's formula.

There is a catch, though. The stock market indexes are created from stocks of companies that are already successful and have a long track record of operational performance. The basket of crypto you want to hold is based on start-ups, many of which may not succeed. And there will be those who are not born yet. Think as if you invested in Myspace and watched it get gobbled by Facebook, or you invested in the search engine AltaVista which got hammered by Google. There are several alternative ways to deal with such a problem.

You might hold the top ten (or more) cryptocurrencies by market capitalization in the simplest scenario. Beyond the obvious benefits of diversification, you also invest in momentum because the relatively large market cap of these cryptocurrencies means the momentum is behind them. However, this approach misses an interesting source of return in cryptocurrencies.

You are investing in crypto because you want to invest in start-ups that have large potential upside. By investing in the largest market cap cryptocurrencies, you are missing the potential to invest in smaller market cap cryptocurrencies which can provide you with higher returns as they have more room to grow. I am thinking of the people who complain about missing the bus on bitcoin without realizing that in crypto buses, there are plenty. If you missed bitcoin, you could have bought ether. Had you missed that bus, too, you could have gotten into Solana, then Terra or Polkadot.

The problem is investing in crypto feels like making decisions while your roller coaster ride is about to fall off its peak. You will always be anxious, no matter where the prices are. It's just human nature.

The best way to deal with such a problem is to decide beforehand what you will do under each possible scenario. Imagine all possibilities and then develop a course of action under all those possibilities. Do this before you get on the roller coaster, then, once you are on, simply follow the instructions you wrote for yourself.

Index investing is one such approach that has a theoretical basis behind it, meaning it is supported by data and research.

We can take a similar approach in crypto.

One way to solve this problem is to identify various sectors in crypto and pick a few top coins by market cap in each sector. This approach provides you with further diversification, as individual sector correlations should go down in the long-term. Additionally, you end up investing in smaller cap coins as new sectors emerge. These coins are still at the top of their sector by market cap, which means they also have the wind behind their sails. Is this a good approach? Let data answer this question.

We created seven portfolios with 54 percent Vanguard Total World Stock ETF (VT), 36 percent Vanguard Total Bond Market (BND), and 10 percent in each of the indexes below. The following table shows the performances of these portfolios.

	Annual Return Percent	Annual Volatility Percent	Sharpe Ratio	Maximum Drawdown Percent
BTC	21.66	12.63	1.14	-25.21
Crypto 10—Market Cap Weighted	23.42	12.55	1.22	-25.22
Crypto 10—Equally Weighted	34.05	15.31	1.40	-27.39
Crypto 10—Top Two by Sector—Market Cap Weighted	23.16	12.45	1.22	-24.92
Crypto 100—Top Ten by Sector—Market Cap Weighted	23.37	12.50	1.22	-25.01
Crypto 10—Top Two by Sector—Equally Weighted	**35.50**	**15.75**	**1.41**	**-26.75**
Crypto 100—Top Ten by Sector—Equally Weighted	39.55	18.69	1.32	-27.98

Performance Statistics of Crypto Strategies Combined with a Traditional Portfolio; Source: Quantuna.com

The duration used is from January 1, 2016, to September 30, 2021. I chose this duration because many of the sectors had not developed before. It was only after the launch of Ethereum in 2015 that many sectors driven by the development of dApps emerged.

The sectors chosen were currency, smart contract platform, DeFi, exchange tokens, and gaming.

Indexes are created as follows:

BTC: Buy and hold bitcoin.

Crypto 10—Market Cap Weighted: Top ten cryptocurrencies by market capitalization, weighted by their market cap, rebalanced monthly.

Crypto 10—Equally Weighted: Top ten cryptocurrencies by market capitalization, equally weighted, rebalanced monthly.

Crypto 10—Top Two by Sector—Market Cap Weighted: Top two cryptocurrencies ranked by market capitalization, from five sectors, weighted by their market cap, new capital added every month, not rebalanced.

Crypto 50—Top Ten by Sector—Market Cap Weighted: Top ten cryptocurrencies ranked by market capitalization, from five sectors, weighted by their market cap, new capital added every month, not rebalanced.

Crypto 10—Top Two by Sector—Equally Weighted: Top two cryptocurrencies ranked by market capitalization, from five sectors, equally weighted, new capital added every month, not rebalanced.

Crypto 50—Top Ten by Sector—Equally Weighted: Top ten cryptocurrencies ranked by market capitalization, from five sectors, equally weighted, new capital added every month, not rebalanced.

ANALYZING THE RESULTS

An interesting result of the above analysis is **equally weighted versions performed much better than the market cap weighted version of each index.** The returns and Sharpe ratio (SR) are significantly higher for the equally weighted version.

This is most likely due to the size effect. By choosing top cryptocurrencies by market cap we are selecting coins with relatively high quality. By equally weighing the coins, we are giving smaller coins the same weight as larger coins. The smaller coins have more room to grow. This enhances the return compared to a market cap weighted approach.

We can also see the Sharpe ratio is highest for Crypto 10—Top Two by Sector—Equally Weighted, closely followed by Crypto 10—Equally Weighted.

However, **Crypto 10—Top Two by Sector—Equally Weighted is easier to manage, as we do not sell any coins, but add them every month based on the new set of coins that month satisfying the criteria of the index.** This should also reduce cost, as we trade less. We have not considered costs in this analysis. It is known the trading costs can have a significant impact on portfolio returns.

Crypto 10—Top Two by Sector—Equally Weighted has an additional benefit. By not selling any coins, you are creating a VC-type portfolio where you hold your coins for the long-term. You add positions, not reduce them as you would do with a standard index. Given cryptocurrency investments are investments in start-ups, **you end up getting the benefit of both VC-type portfolios by using a Wall Street-type index.**

Here is a chart of the cumulative multiple returns of Crypto 10—Top Two by Sector—Equally Weighted, bitcoin (BTC), and Crypto 10—Market Cap Weighted. Bitcoin and market cap weighted indexes are commonly offered funds in the market. If you initially invested one dollar or one currency unit, cumulative multiple returns in these graphs show the value of that investment with time.

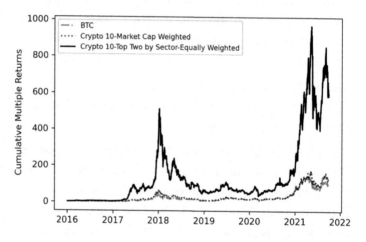

Cumulative Multiple Returns of Three Crypto Strategies;
Source: Quantuna.com

To mimic this basket, choose five sectors: currency, smart contract platform, DeFi, exchange tokens, and gaming. At the beginning of each month, select the top two cryptocurrencies in each sector, giving you a total of ten cryptocurrencies. Divide your investment equally in these ten crypto. A minimum of ten dollars would be needed to buy each cryptocurrency on an exchange like Coinbase, as they set a minimum trade size. This would lead to a minimum investment of one hundred dollars each month.

In five years, this index would have beaten both BTC and Crypto 10—Market Cap Weighted by wide margins. The cumulative return multiple in the graph shows you roughly how many times your initial investment (on day one) would have grown with time. In the final week of September 2021, you would have the following cumulative return multiples:

BTC: 97X.

Crypto 10—Market Cap Weighted: 125X.

Crypto 10—Top Two by Sector—Equally Weighted: 597X.

In US dollars, starting from January 1, 2016, the value of the third strategy, in the last week of September 2021, would be:

Crypto 10—Top Two by Sector—Equally Weighted: 360 thousand dollars.

On a total investment of sixty-nine hundred dollars.

You can't argue with numbers!

Conclusion

———

"Out of intense complexities, intense simplicities emerge."

—WINSTON CHURCHILL

At this point in the book, you have accomplished a lot. You went on a journey covering the past seven decades of innovation that brought us the Web 3.0. We are on the cusp of the next technological breakthrough, which will reorganize the Internet by taking out centralized players like banks, trading exchanges, and social media companies who have captured most of the value created by the masses on the Internet and Web 2.0. With Web 3.0, the middlemen will be out, and the masses will be in—that means you.

As we saw in many examples of DeFi, people will be paid in cryptocurrencies to participate in the networks they help grow. The next time you log into your social media account and write a story or post a picture, think about that for a moment. That like from your friend on the picture of your cute puppy just helped Instagram monetarily by making its network more valuable. What if there was a decentralized version of Instagram where you owned the content you created and got paid in tokens every time someone liked it? Would you like to be paid for posting content on Instagram or trading on a decentralized exchange? The economics of cryptocurrencies are too attractive for users to ignore.

If anything, we are still in the early phases of the blockchain revolution. If you are still undecided about cryptocurrencies as an investment, it is time for you to buy your first ten dollars' worth. No matter how small your investment is, your mind will follow your money. With that, you will gain experience, wisdom, and a deeper appreciation of the knowledge from this book.

If you are already deep in this asset class, you should reevaluate your decisions using the tools and framework developed in this book. It will give you a better, more intelligent approach to design your portfolio.

You are now equipped with the knowledge of history, technology, and qualitative and analytical tools that will be more than sufficient for taking a plunge in this exciting, wealth-building opportunity that was never available to so many before.

The journey of cryptocurrencies has been straight to the moon. However, don't worry if you have missed a few buses on the crypto junction. Another one will be coming soon. This time, you are well equipped to hop on your way to financial riches.

Acknowledgments

I want to thank my family, especially my parents, Sri Krishna Sharma and Malti Sharma, without whose faith, love, and support, I would not be here. Thanks to my wife, Aparna, and children, Agastya and Aryan, for being patient with me throughout the book writing. Thanks to my brothers, Anoop and Atul, for always loving me and standing by me—and their family, Priyanka, Namrata, Myra, and Avyan, for helping me build a home away from home.

I want to thank my grandfather, Sri Satyendra Sharma, who became my inspiration from early on. I have come a long way just by looking up to him.

Special thanks to Haoliang (Billy) Zheng for helping with research, Anoop Kaushik for creating code for calculating indices, Vishal Bajpayee for sourcing data, and the team at Quantuna.com for providing charts.

I want to thank the following individuals for reading my book and giving me valuable feedback. The book has improved a lot with your comments.

Anuj Kumar
Executive Director, Quantitative Research, JPMorgan Chase

Ravi Srivastava
Cofounder and Managing Partner, Purvi Capital LLC

Shashwat Shah
Vice President, Goldman Sachs

Siddharth Gupta
Senior Portfolio Manager, New Holland Capital

Vikas Goela
Vice President, Goldman Sachs

Vishal Bajpayee
Senior Software Developer, BGC Partners

Thanks to interviewees Mike Novogratz, Matt Hougan, Rich Rosenblum, Geoff Kendrick, Manuel Ernesto De Luque Muntaner, Suzanne Ley, Dr. Prash Puspanathan, and Mark van Rijmenam.

I want to thank everyone at Creators Institute, particularly Eric Koester and David Grandouiller, and everybody at the New Degree Press, especially Brian Bies and my editors, Cynthia Tucker and Linda Berardelli, for helping me throughout the process. Without them, this book would not be possible. Thanks to Slaviša Živković, my layout editor, for creating a beautiful book.

The following people supported me through the presale campaign of my book. I want to thank them for their support in helping spread the word.

Abash Lal
Abhay Bhaskar
Abhay Singh
Ajay Hariharan
Akesh Bhalla
Akshaya Sharma
Alok Srivastava
Amit Singh
Amit Sinha
Anand Agarwal
Ankit Shukla
Anoop Kaushik
Anuj Kumar
Aparna Agarwal
Apratim Rajendra
Apratim Rajendra
Arshpreet Kaur
Arvind Kalra
Ashwini Kumar
Atul Kaushik
Babita Gupta
Boris Novakov
Borun Chowdhury
Cynthia Tucker
David Hughes
Deepak jain
Eric Koester

Eshwar Mysore
Gauranga Pal
Girish Mallapragada
Glenn Veralli
Hassan Tariq
Henry Liu
Himanshu Shekhar
Jagrati Shringi
Jawahar Lal
Jerome Loman
Jimmy Samaha
Kalyan Rokkam
Kartik Sahni
Krishna Chandra
Mamta Saksena
Marek Laboutka
Mukul Tripathi
Nama Virmani
Namrata Dwivedi
Naval Mehrotra
Naveen Dachuri
Nicolas Diener
Nikhil Sharma
Nirmit Joshi
Nishant Sharma
Vivek Agarwal
Nitin Agarwal

Pradeep Chand

Pradyot Prakash

Pranav Tripathi

Pranjal Thakur

Priyanka Sharma

Puneet Srivastava

Rajeshwari Chakravarty

Rajiv Bhat

Ram Misra

Ramesh Gupta

Randeep Singh

Ratan Bajpai

Ravi Chandra Ragampeta

Ravi Srivastava

Ritesh Agarwal

Robert Park

Rohit Singh

Rudrapriya Subudhi

Rui Wang

Shree Bharadwaj

Sabyasachi Chakravarty

Sachin Sancheti

Sachin Shah

Samarth Rastogi

Sanjeev Kumar

Savr Enkeev

Shankar Mishra

Shantanu Sharma

Shashidhar Upadhyay

Shashwat Shah

Shreesh Mishra

Shridhar Sivaraman

Siddhartha Gupta

Snehamoy Mukherjee

Sonu Sonkar

Sooraj Mohan Saksena

Srikrishna Sharma Kaushik

Stuti Saksena Sahni

Sunil Agarwal

Sunit Mayank

Suzanne Ley

Tamhant Jain

Tapan Singh Pratihar

Tim James

Vijay Kumar Agarwal

Vikas Goela

Vikas Navik

Vimal Kumar

Vinay Chauhan

Vincent Godreuil

Vipin Singh

Vishal Bajpayee

CHAPTER 1: WHERE SILICON VALLEY MEETS WALL STREET

Erickson, Christine. "Facebook IPO: The Complete Guide." *Mashable,* February 3, 2012. https://mashable.com/2012/02/03/facebook-ipo-complete-guide/.

Hoffman, Claire. "The Battle for Facebook." *RollingStone,* September 15, 2010. https://www.rollingstone.com/culture/culture-news/the-battle-for-facebook-242989/.

Isidore, Chris. "Mark Zuckerberg's net worth falls by $7.2 billion." *CNN Money,* July 27, 2012. https://money.cnn.com/2012/07/27/technology/zuckerberg-net-worth/index.htm.

Kirkpatrick, David. *"The Facebook Effect: The Inside Story of the Company That Is Connecting the World."* New York. Simon & Schuster: 2011.

Pepitone, Julianne, and Stacy Cowley. "Facebook's first big investor, Peter Thiel, crashes out." *CNN Business,* August 20, 2012. https://money.cnn.com/2012/08/20/technology/facebook-peter-thiel/index.html

Rusli, Evelyn M., and Peter Eavis. *New York Times,* May 17, 2012. https://dealbook.nytimes.com/2012/05/17/facebook-raises-16-billion-in-i-p-o/?hp.

CHAPTER 2: BITCOIN VS. BITCOIN

Andreessen, Marc. "Why Bitcoin Matters." *The New York Times,* Jan 21, 2014. https://dealbook.nytimes.com/2014/01/21/why-bitcoin-matters/.

Board of Governors of the Federal Reserve System. "Credit and Liquidity Programs and the Balance Sheet." Accessed October 10, 2021. https://www.federalreserve.gov/monetarypolicy/bst_recenttrends.htm.

Appendix

INTRODUCTION

Crippen, Alex. "Bitcoin and cryptocurrencies." *CNBC*, June 26, 2018. https://buffett.cnbc.com/2018/06/26/buffett-a-z-bitcoinand-cryptocurrencies.html.

Schatzker, Erik. "How Mike Novogratz Got Hooked on Cryptocurrencies." *Bloomberg*, September 26, 2017. https://www.bloomberg.com/news/videos/2017-09-26/h mike-novogratz-got-hooked-on-cryptocurrencies-vide

Son, Hugh. "Goldman Sachs is close to offering bitcoin an other digital assets to its wealth management clients." *CNBC*, March 31, 2021. https://www.cnbc.com/2021/0 bitcoin-goldman-is-close-to-offering-bitcoin-to-its-clients.html.

Young, Joseph. "Goldman Sachs Tells Clients Bitcoin Good, But It Seems to Secretly Like It." *Forbes*, Ji 2020. https://www.forbes.com/sites/youngjoseph/202 goldman-sachs-tells-clients-bitcoin-isnt-good-to-secretly-like-it/?sh=6dfceecd1362.

Damodaran, Aswath. "The Bitcoin Boom: Asset, Currency, Commodity or Collectible?" *Musings on Markets* (blog). October 24, 2017. https://aswathdamodaran.blogspot.com/2017/10/the-bitcoin-boom-asset-currency.html.

Damodaran, Aswath. "The Cryptocurrency Debate: Future of Money or Speculative Hype" *Musings on Markets* (blog). August 1, 2017.

https://aswathdamodaran.blogspot.com/2017/08/the-crypto-currency-debate-future-of.html

Markowitz, Harry. "Portfolio Selection." *The Journal of Finance,* Vol. 7, No. 1. (Mar, 1952): 77–91.

Mehrling, Perry G. "Economics of Money and Banking." Columbia University. New York. Last accessed October 20, 2021. coursera.org/learn/money-banking.

The World Bank. "Financial Inclusion on the Rise, But Gaps Remain, global Findex Database Shows." April 19, 2018. https://www.worldbank.org/en/news/press-release/2018/04/19/financial-inclusion-on-the-rise-but-gaps-remain-global-findex-database-shows.

Wright, Turner. "Bitfinex Made a $1.1 Billion BTC Transaction for only $0.68." *Cointelegraph.* April 13, 2020. https://cointelegraph.com/news/bitfinex-made-a-11-billion-btc-transaction-for-only-068.

CHAPTER 3: A BRAVE NEW WORLD

Gromov, Gregory. "Roads and Crossroads of the Internet History." Last Updated 2012. https://history-of-internet.com/

Iansiti, Marco and Karim R. Lakhani. "The Truth About Blockchain." *Harvard Business Review* 95, no. 1 (January–February 2017): 118–127.

Perry, Mark J. "Only 52 US Companies have been on the Fortune 500 since 1955, thanks to the creative destruction that fuels economic prosperity." Carpe-Diem. American Enterprise Institute. May 22, 2019.

https://www.aei.org/carpe-diem/only-52-us-companies-have-been-on-the-fortune-500-since-1955-thanks-to-the-creative-destruction-that-fuels-economic-prosperity/.

Quinn, William, and John D. Turner. *Boom and Bust: A Global History of Bubbles*. Cambridge, U.K. Cambridge University Press: 2020.

Schumpeter, Joseph A. "Capitalism, Socialism, and Democracy." New York. Harper & Row, 1962.

CHAPTER 4: THE CRYPTO ANARCHY OF CYPHERPUNKS

Back, Adam. "A partial hash collision-based postage scheme." Last updated March 28, 1997. http://www.hashcash.org/papers/announce.txt.

Chaum, David. "Untraceable Electronic Mail, Return Addresses, and Digital Pseudonyms." *Communications of the ACM,* 24 (2) (1981): 84–90.

Dai, Wei. "b-money." Accessed October 10, 2021. http://www.weidai.com/bmoney.txt.

Finney, Hall. "16 August 2004. Hal Finney extends his invitation to everyone." Accessed October 10, 2021. https://cryptome.org/rpow.htm.

Hughes, Eric. "A Cypherpunk's Manifesto." Last updated March 9, 1993. https://www.activism.net/cypherpunk/manifesto.html.

Levy, Steven. "Battle of the Clipper Chip." *New York Times Magazine.* July 12, 1994. https://www.nytimes.com/1994/06/12/magazine/battle-of-the-clipper-chip.html.

Levy, Steven. "Crypto Rebels." *Wired,* Feb 1, 1993. https://www.wired.com/1993/02/crypto-rebels/.

Qureshi, Haseeb. "The Cypherpunks." Last updated Dec 29, 2019. https://nakamoto.com/the-cypherpunks/.

Szabo, Nick.B" December 2005.
https://unenumerated.blogspot.com/2005/12/bit-gold.html.

Zimmermann, Philip. "Why I wrote PGP." Last updated 1999.
http://www.philzimmermann.com/EN/essays/
WhyIWrotePGP.html.

CHAPTER 5: BITCOIN: THE INTERNET MONEY

Elliott, Francis, and Duncan, Gary.C" *The Times,* January
3, 2009. https://www.thetimes.co.uk/article/chancellor-
alistair-darling-on-brink-of-second-bailout-for-banks-
n9l382mn62h.

Foley, Stephen. "Greenspan says crisis left him in 'shocked disbelief.'"
Independent, October 23, 2011.
https://www.independent.co.uk/news/business/news/greenspan-
says-crisis-left-him-in-shocked-disbelief-971609.html.

Lin, Rustie, and Gloria Wang. "Bitcoin and Cryptocurrencies."
University of California, Berkeley, CA. October 2021.
https://www.edx.org/course/bitcoin-and-cryptocurrencies.

Nakamoto, Satoshi. "Bitcoin: A Peer-to-Peer Electronic Cash
System." October 31, 2008. https://bitcoin.org/bitcoin.pdf.

Wharton. Guillen, Mauro F. "The Global Economic & Financial
Crisis: A Timeline." June, 2015.
https://lauder.wharton.upenn.edu/wp-content/
uploads/2015/06/Chronology_Economic_Financial_Crisis.pdf.

CHAPTER 6: ETHEREUM: THE WORLD COMPUTER

Finley, Klint. "Out in the Open: Teenage Hacker Transforms
Web into One Giant Bitcoin Network." *WIRED.* January 27,
2014. https://www.wired.com/2014/01/ethereum/.

Gemini Trust Company, LLC. "Ethereum and the ICO Boom."
Last Modified May 27, 2021. Accessed October 20, 2021.
https://www.gemini.com/cryptopedia/initial-coin-offering-
explained-ethereum-ico#section-ethereums-role-in-the-
ico-boom.

Kauflin, Jeff. "Where Did the Money Go? Inside the Big Crypto ICOs of 2017." *Forbes.* October 29, 2018. https://www.forbes.com/sites/jeffkauflin/2018/10/29/where-did-the-money-go-inside-the-big-crypto-icos-of-2017/?sh=437d4349261b.

Mims, Christopher. "New Research Busts Popular Myths About Innovation." *The Wall Street Journal.* September 18, 2021. https://www.wsj.com/articles/new-research-busts-popular-myths-about-innovation-11631937693.

Naumoff, Alicia. "Exclusive Interview with Vitalik Buterin: Ethereum, Bitcoin, ICO & More." *Cointelegraph.* April 13, 2017. https://cointelegraph.com/news/exclusive-interview-with-vitalik-buterin-ethereum-bitcoin-ico-more.

Paumgarten, Nick. "The Prophets of Cryptocurrency Survey the Boom and Dust." *The New Yorker.* October 15, 2018. https://www.newyorker.com/magazine/2018/10/22/the-prophets-of-cryptocurrency-survey-the-boom-and-bust.

Peck, Morgan. "The Uncanny Mind That Built Ethereum." Backchannel. *Wired.* June 13, 2016. https://www.wired.com/2016/06/the-uncanny-mind-that-built-ethereum/.

Russell, John. "Former Mozilla CEO raises $35M in under 30 seconds for his browser startup Brave." *TechCrunch.* June 1, 2017. https://techcrunch.com/2017/06/01/brave-ico-35-million-30-seconds-brendan-eich/.

Szabo, Nick (September 1997). "Formalizing and Securing Relationships on Public Networks." *First Monday.* 2 (9). doi:10.5210/fm.v2i9.548. Retrieved 8 January 2017.

CHAPTER 7: DECENTRALIZED APPLICATIONS

Alexandre, Ana. "Andreessen Horowitz Invests $15 Million in Stablecoin Firm MakerDAO." *Cointelegraph.* September 25, 2018. https://cointelegraph.com/news/andreessen-horowitz-invests-15-million-in-stablecoin-firm-makerdao.

Browne, Ryan. "Cryptocurrency firms Tether and Bitfinex agree to pay $18.5 million fine to end New York probe." *CNBC*, February 23, 2021. https://www.cnbc.com/2021/02/23/tether-bitfinex-reach-settlement-with-new-york-attorney-general.html.

Dale, Brady. "MakerDAO Moves to Full Decentralization; Maker Foundation to Close in 'Months.'" *Coindesk*, Last Updated, September 14, 2021. https://www.coindesk.com/tech/2021/07/20/makerdao-moves-to-full-decentralization-maker-foundation-to-close-in-months/.

Gemini Trust Company, LLC. "What iIs MakerDAO." Last Modified March 12, 2021. Accessed October 20, 2021. https://www.gemini.com/cryptopedia/makerdao-dai-decentralized-autonomous-organization#section-dai-not-the-only-stablecoin-but-the-most-ubiquitous.

Gemini Trust Company, LLC. "How MakerDAO Pioneered Decentralized Finance." Last Modified March 12, 2021. Accessed October 20, 2021. https://www.gemini.com/cryptopedia/makerdao-defi-mkr-dai-coins.

Hankin, Aaron.N" *Fortune*. February 26, 2018. https://www.marketwatch.com/story/nearly-half-of-all-2017-icos-have-failed-2018-02-26.

CHAPTER 8: A TALE OF TWO ECONOMIES

Arthur, W. Brian."Increasing Returns and the New World of Business." *Harvard Business Review*, July–August, 1996. https://hbr.org/1996/07/increasing-returns-and-the-new-world-of-business.

Flinley, Klint. "Was Microsoft's Empire Built on Stolen Code? We May Never Know." *Wired.* Aug 7, 2012. https://www.wired.com/2012/08/ms-dos-examined-for-thef/.

"Gary Kildall The DOS that wasn't." *Forbes*, 1997. https://www.forbes.com/forbes/1997/0707/6001336a.html?sh=23f31c40140e.

Greene, Jay, and Steve Hamm. "The Man Who Could Have Been Bill Gates." *Bloomberg Businessweek*, October 25, 2004. https://www.bloomberg.com/news/articles/2004-10-24/the-man-who-could-have-been-bill-gates.

CHAPTER 9: NETWORK, NETWORK, NETWORK

Walden, Jesse. "Crypto's Business Model is Familiar. What Isn't is Who Benefits." Last Updated April 10, 2020. Accessed October 10, 2020. https://jessewalden.com/cryptos-business-model-is-familiar-what-isnt-is-who-benefits-2/.

Young, Martin. "Compound Finance founder says that CeFi will embrace DeFi." *Cointelegraph.* December 16, 2020. https://cointelegraph.com/news/compound-finance-founder-says-that-cefi-will-embrace-defi.

Zhu, Feng, and Marco Iansiti. "*Why Some Platforms Thrive and Others* Don't." *Harvard Business Review* 97, no. 1 (January–February 2019): 118–125.

CHAPTER 10: DISRUPTIVE INNOVATION

Bower, J. L., and C. M. Christensen. "Disruptive Technologies: Catching the Wave." *Harvard Business Review* 73, no. 1 (January–February 1995): 43–53.

Ryan, Greg. "Visa CEO is all about tech. But blockchain and bitcoin? Not right now." *Boston Business Journal.* September 27, 2018. https://www.bizjournals.com/boston/news/2018/09/27/visa-ceo-is-all-about-tech-but-blockchain-and.html.

CHAPTER 11: A TECH DÉJÀ VU

Andreessen, Marc. "Why Software Is Eating the World." *The Wall Street Journal*, April 20, 2011. https://www.wsj.com/articles/SB10001424053111903480904576512250915629460.

Andreessen, Marc. "Why Bitcoin Matters." *The New York Times*, Jan 21, 2014. https://dealbook.nytimes.com/2014/01/21/why-bitcoin-matters/.

Blosch, Marcus and Jackie Fenn. "Understanding Gartner's Hype Cycles." *Gartner Research*, Aug 20.2018. https://www.gartner.com/en/documents/3887767.

Clifford, Catherine. "Warren Buffett on Not investing in Amazon—and why it's not his biggest mistake." *CNBC*, May 1, 2019. https://www.cnbc.com/2019/05/01/warren-buffett-on-not-investing-in-amazon.html.

Friend, Tad. "Tomorrow's Advance Men." *The New Yorker*, May 11, 2015. https://www.newyorker.com/magazine/2015/05/18/tomorrows-advance-man#.

The Time Magazine, Feb, 1996, http://content.time.com/time/covers/0,16641,19960219,00.html.

CHAPTER 12: A VALUATION CONUNDRUM

Damodaran, Aswath. "On the Uber Rollercoaster: Narrative Tweaks, Twists and Turns!" *Musings on Markets* (blog). October 2, 2015. http://aswathdamodaran.blogspot.com/2015/10/on-uber-rollercoaster-narrative-tweaks.html.

Damodaran, Aswath. "Uber Isn't Worth $17 Billion." *FiveThirtyEight*. June 18, 2014. https://fivethirtyeight.com/features/uber-isnt-worth-17-billion/.

Damodaran, Aswath. "Up, up and away! A crowd-valuation of Uber!" *Musings on Markets* (blog). December 2, 2014. http://aswathdamodaran.blogspot.com/2014/12/up-up-and-away-crowd-valuation-of-uber.html.

Gompers, Paul, Will Gornall, Steven N. Kaplan, and Ilya A. Strebulaev. "How Venture Capitalists Make Decisions Works." *Harvard Business Review*. March-April, 2021. https://hbr.org/2021/03/how-venture-capitalists-make-decisions.

Graham, Alex. "Three Core Principles of Venture Capital Portfolio Strategy." Toptal. Accessed October 21, 2021. https://www.toptal.com/finance/venture-capital-consultants/venture-capital-portfolio-strategy.

Gurley, Bill. "How to Miss By a Mile: An Alternative Look at Uber's Potential Market Size." *Above the Crowd* (blog). July 11, 2014. https://abovethecrowd.com/2014/07/11/how-to-miss-by-a-mile-an-alternative-look-at-ubers-potential-market-size/.

Johnson, Joseph. "Worldwide digital population as of January 2021." *Statista.* September 10, 2021.

Macmillan, Douglas, Sam Schechner, and Lisa Fleisher. "Uber Snags $41 Valuation." *The Wall Street Journal.* Updated December 5, 2014. https://www.wsj.com/articles/ubers-new-funding-values-it-at-over-41-billion-1417715938.

Zider, Bob. "How Venture Capital Works." *Harvard Business Review.* November-December, 1998. https://hbr.org/1998/11/how-venture-capital-works.

CHAPTER 13: VALUATION OF CRYPTOCURRENCIES

Copeland, Tim. "Decentralized finance is now a $200 billion industry." *The Block,* October 13, 2020. https://www.theblockcrypto.com/post/120379/decentralized-finance-is-now-a-200-billion-industry?utm_source=telegram&utm_medium=social.

Kendrick, Geoff, Christopher Graham, and Melissa Chan. "Bitcoin Investor Guide." Standard Chartered Bank. September 7, 2021.

Kendrick, Geoff, Christopher Graham, and Melissa Chan. "Ethereum Investor Guide." Standard Chartered Bank. September 7, 2021.

Miller IV, Bill, and Bill Miller. "The Value Investor's Case for... Bitcoin?!" *Miller Value Partners.* September 8, 2015. https://millervalue.com/a-value-investors-case-for-bitcoin/

Miller IV, Bill, and Tyler Grason. "Microstrategy and Bitcoin: The Mother of All Fat Tails?" *Miller Value Partners*. January 21, 2021. https://millervalue.com/4q20-income-strategy-letter/

CHAPTER 14: THE CRYPTO OPPORTUNITY

Kahneman, Daniel, and Amos Tversky. "Prospect Theory: An Analysis of Decision under Risk." *Econometrica,* Vol. 47, No. 2 (Mar., 1979): 263–292.

Levy, Rachel and Liz Hoffman. "SoftBank Founder Masayoshi Son Lost $130 Million on Bitcoin." *The Wall Street Journal.* April 23, 2019. https://www.wsj.com/articles/softbank-founder-masayoshi-son-lost-130-million-on-bitcoin-11556017200.

Li, Shine. "Crypto Bull Anthony Pompliano Reveals That 80% of His Wealth Is Bitcoin." *Blockchain News.* October 19, 2020. https://blockchain.news/news/crypto-bull-anthony-pompliano-reveals-80-wealth-is-bitcoin.

CHAPTER 16: CRYPTO IN A PORTFOLIO

Hougan, Matt and David Lawant. "*The Guide to Bitcoin, Blockchain, And Cryptocurrency for Investment Professionals.*" CFA Institute Research Foundation. 2021.

CHAPTER 17: INVESTING IN CRYPTOCURRENCIES

Harvey, Campbell R., Ashwin Ramachandran, and Joey Santoro. *DeFi and The Future of Finance.* Hoboken. New Jersey. Wiley: 2021.